THE ACCIDENTAL SALESPERSON

SECOND EDITION

Jack Brownlee

THE ACCIDENTAL SALESPERSON

How to Take Control of Your Sales Career and Earn the Respect and Income You Deserve

SECOND EDITION

CHRIS LYTLE

AMACOM

American Management Association

New York • Atlanta • Brussels • Chicago • Mexico City • San Francisco
Shanghai • Tokyo • Toronto • Washington, D.C.

Bulk discounts available. For details visit:
www.amacombooks.org/go/specialsales
Or contact special sales:
Phone: 800-250-5308
E-mail: specialsls@amanet.org
View all the AMACOM titles at: www.amacombooks.org

This publication is designed to provide accurate and authoritative information
in regard to the subject matter covered. It is sold with the understanding
that the publisher is not engaged in rendering legal, accounting, or other
professional service. If legal advice or other expert assistance is required,
the services of a competent professional person should be sought.

Library of Congress Cataloging-in-Publication Data
Lytle, Chris.
   The accidental salesperson : how to take control of your sales career and
earn the respect and income you deserve / Chris Lytle.—2nd ed.
       p. cm.
   Includes bibliographical references and index.
   ISBN-13: 978-0-8144-3086-6 (alk. paper)
   ISBN-10: 0-8144-3086-4 (alk. paper)
1. Selling. 2. Success in business. I. Title.
   HF5438.25.L93 2012
   658.8'102--dc23   2012007694

About AMA
American Management Association (www.amanet.org) is a world leader in
talent development, advancing the skills of individuals to drive business
success. Our mission is to support the goals of individuals and organizations
through a complete range of products and services, including classroom and
virtual seminars, webcasts, webinars, podcasts, conferences, corporate and
government solutions, business books, and research. AMA's approach to
improving performance combines experiential learning—learning through
doing—with opportunities for ongoing professional growth at every step of
one's career journey.

Printing number
10 9 8 7 6

CONTENTS

AUTHOR'S NOTE
FOR THE SECOND EDITION

Shortly after the publication of the first edition of *The Accidental Salesperson*, I got a call from a salesperson who was clearly agitated. "I need some sales training," he told me.

Practicing what I preach, I began to ask him questions.

"Why today?" I asked. "What prompted you to call me today instead of last week or two weeks from now?"

He answered: "Well, I've only been on the job for a few months and I just made the biggest sale in our company's history."

"Congratulations. But why do you need sales training if you're setting records?" (It's been my experience that most of my customers purchase sales training after a missed quota or a bad quarter. Yet this guy was a rising star in his company.)

"Thanks," he said, accepting the compliment. "But now the owners of the company and my boss want bigger sales, and I have no idea how or why I made that sale."

Sales success can be stressful if you don't know how to repeat it.

You can get into sales accidentally and you can accidentally make sales. But successful salespeople and sales organizations, including companies I have had the privilege of working with, have all had a repeatable sales process. They know what works and why it works.

Once you have read and applied the lessons in this book, you too will have a repeatable, dependable sales process. That's because *The Accidental Salesperson* adds the structure missing from so many sales books, videos, CDs, and training events.

One VP of sales for a billion-dollar company told me that he buys copies of *The Accidental Salesperson* by the boxful and distributes them to his new hires. And salespeople often call, write, and e-mail me to let me know that reading the book has changed their lives by helping them do what the subtitle promises—take control of their careers and earn the respect and income they deserve. (There's a big difference between a signed personal letter and an e-mail, as you will discover in Chapter 7, "Getting In to See Anybody.")

A lot has changed about selling in the thirteen years since I turned in my manuscript for the first edition. For instance, you may be selling to a buying committee instead of a single decision maker. Also, the Internet gives your buyers access to a tremendous amount of information that salespeople used to provide. Salespeople now have their own websites. And while I have yet to meet a salesperson who has ever sold anything by spending time on Facebook, lots of us have connected with customers and prospects on LinkedIn and other networking sites.

Face-to-face meetings, while more important than ever, seem harder to come by. That's why in Chapter 5, I recommend a new "magic question" to help you get your unfair share of these meetings.

Preparation in advance of the meeting is as important as ever, but it's easier than ever before as well. You can research people and companies easily and effortlessly with just a few keystrokes. Believe it or not, the first edition of this book was published before *Google* was a verb. Google was founded in 1998, a year before I sent my first manuscript to AMACOM.

The ideas from the first edition that hold up the best involve having a systematic approach to everything. By "everything" I mean you need a system for . . .

- Generating leads and inquiries
- Getting the first face-to-face meeting or telephone meeting with a prospect
- Weeding out prospects from information seekers
- Keeping the sale open long enough to get it closed

- Writing and making proposals (the shorter the better, and I explain why in Chapter 10.

- Confirming the sale (and I contend you don't have a business relationship with a person until that person, or that person's comptroller, writes you a check)

- Following up and growing the relationship

In the second edition, you will find brand-new information about each of those systems within the selling process. There are also two new tools. The Proposal Producer takes you by the hand and shows you how to take data you have already gathered and turn them into a client-focused proposal. The Platinum Service Checklist prompts you to follow up after the sale with a systematic series of "touches," my goal being to show you how to build relationships your competitors can't steal.

In addition, you'll find an all-new Chapter 11, "Making Your Presentation Like a Pro," where I share tips and tricks I have picked up in twenty-eight years of professional speaking so that you, too, will know how to make powerful, memorable presentations and close more sales. Making just a few subtle refinements in your presentations can position you as an authority to be reckoned with.

And, finally, it has become increasingly clear to me, from my firsthand experience delivering speeches and writing about selling, that closing sales is not really the purpose of selling. In Chapter 15, I challenge you to sell on purpose and with purpose.

All of the tools in this book are posted at www.sparque.biz/accidentalsp as well, where you can download everything of interest to you. This is especially helpful for those of you who purchased this title on your Kindle or other electronic reader. You'll want to get the forms and tools full-size from the website.

The underlying philosophy of the first book has stood the test of time. Customers want to do business with the very best salespeople. They want to be challenged with new information and presented with business-building ideas. They want engaging meetings with well-prepared salespeople. More than ever, they need salespeople who can show them how to grow the sales of their own businesses, hold on to their existing customers, and/or streamline their business processes. It is these salespeople who will win the business of demanding customers.

Today, to succeed in sales you need knowledge, skills, and the proper attitude. In this book you will get all three in abundance.

July 12, 2011
Chicago

INTRODUCTION

Do You Believe in Destiny?

It is no accident you picked up this book. You may not have chosen sales as a profession; it may have chosen you. That applies to most of us. It is why *The Accidental Salesperson* title struck a responsive chord with you. You "ended up" in sales instead of planning this career. Now your success depends on your ability to sell your ideas, concepts, processes, and products to others—to sell on purpose, even if you ended up in sales accidentally.

You bring a lifetime of experience to this book. You already have gained plenty of wisdom about what works and what doesn't work in selling. This book will reinforce everything you are doing right. It will gently correct your course where you are off track.

You will quickly internalize the principles of selling on purpose. That's a promise. You won't have to compromise your values or change your personality to benefit. Having a new framework to think about what you do gives you a powerful edge over those accidental salespeople who have yet to embrace a philosophy of selling.

This is not a sales book for dummies. Far from it. It's a book for thinking people who realize they must sell *more* and who want to understand what works in sales today and why it works. Best of all, there are no tricks, techniques, or high-pressure tactics to learn. With a few subtle but powerful refinements in the things you are already doing, your sales can soar. This is a "why to" book filled with principles that work over and over again in selling.

You are about to learn how to take control of the dynamics of a selling situation and leverage every client contact. Very soon, you will be relying on your extraordinary selling skills instead of the e-mailing skills that reactive salespeople rely on. Expect to shorten your selling cycle and slash the number of objections you have to overcome.

That's just the first three chapters.

In the remaining chapters, you are going to learn specific strategies for every stage of the selling process. Occasionally, you may remark to yourself, "I do that already." That's good. My challenge to you is simply to do it more often and do it on purpose.

The Accidental Salesperson is not a survival manual. It is a manifesto for pros who want to thrive in sales. It's a booster shot for propelling plateaued veterans to the next level. It's a starter kit for the recent grad that has just discovered that the best jobs out there are sales jobs.

As a professional speaker, I promise my audiences more usable information per minute than any speaker out there. Well, this book contains more usable information per chapter than anything on the market. All you have to do is read and apply the concepts to your current situation. You don't even have to finish the book before you start applying its principles. Each chapter spotlights a powerful concept that's self-contained and immediately applicable to your very next client contact.

Something Socrates said may help explain why this book will have an impact on you: "I cannot teach anybody anything. I can only make them think." Although Socrates said it in Greek twenty-four centuries or so ago, it is still relevant.

My role is to get you to think about what you are doing and why you are doing it that way. Each chapter suggests specific refinements you can make in the way you do business.

Opportunities abound for salespeople who sell *on purpose*.

To know and not to do is not to know. Education without action is entertainment. While I hope you enjoy the book, understand that it was written for your improvement, not your enjoyment. You can read about a concept today and apply it today. You'll get the most out of *The Accidental Salesperson* by purposefully and immediately applying the concepts.

Every prospect you meet is silently saying, "Show me that you're different."

You are going to show them.

I don't like long good-byes, nor am I fond of long introductions. You are ready to start selling on purpose. So let's begin.

THE ACCIDENTAL SALESPERSON

SECOND EDITION

PART ONE

The Choice . . . the Chart . . .
the Challenge

CHAPTER 1

Making the Choice

It's 11:45 a.m.

A coworker walks into your office or peers over your cubicle wall and says, "I'm hungry."

"Me too. Let's go to lunch," you say.

"Where do you want to go?"

"I don't know. Where do you want to go?"

"What are you hungry for?"

"Nothing special. You decide."

Chances are you have had this conversation recently with a coworker or spouse. With so many restaurants, narrowing the choice to just one becomes a daunting task.

A comedian once joked, "People don't go to Denny's restaurants. They end up there."

They end up there precisely because they begin without a plan. They react to the hunger pang instead of anticipating it. It doesn't occur to some people that they've been getting hungry every four hours of their waking lives. When they finally choose a place to eat, a long line or waiting list often confronts them. As a result, they "end up" settling for something less.

But we're still hungry, so let's get back to the restaurant—any restaurant. Have you ever watched people order? Some people summon the harried waitperson and want her to act as arbiter.

"If you were me, would you have the steak or the fish?" they'll ask, as if one or the other of these portion-controlled entrées would give them a memorable culinary experience.

"Do you like steak or fish better?" says the waitperson, who is forced to do a customer needs analysis to get her 15 percent "commission" out of this sale. Taken to its logical conclusion, the waitperson could be forced to make the choice for the person. "How is your cholesterol, sir? If it's over 200, may I strongly suggest the broiled fish?"

Meanwhile, other customers wait impatiently for their second cup of coffee and mentally deduct a few percentage points from the tip they are planning to leave.

It happens all because it is so hard for some people to make a choice—any choice!

Try this little experiment. Choose a restaurant for lunch a day in advance using just two criteria: 1) Choose a local favorite that is not a chain. 2) Choose a place that takes reservations. Make one choice. Then tell (don't ask) a customer (not a coworker) that you want to take her to lunch. Say, "I've made reservations and I want you to join me at 12:15 p.m. tomorrow afternoon for lunch at The Edgewater, if you don't have other plans."

When you get to the restaurant, look at the menu for five seconds or ignore it altogether. Say, "I'm going to have a cup of the baked onion soup, half a club sandwich, and an iced tea with extra lemon." (Order whatever you feel like having. Just do it decisively.) Prediction: Nine times out of ten your luncheon guest will order two out of the three things you ordered, just because your decisiveness is so comforting and eliminates any need to deliberate further.

Choices are hard for people because they already have too many. There are too many channels on television. There are too many sizes of detergent, too many brands of mustard, too many websites to surf. It's hard enough to choose where you are going to have lunch. Think how much harder it is to choose what you are going to do for a living. The hardest part of all is committing to the choice you've made with all of the career options still available. By making choices quickly and firmly, you position yourself as a decisive, take-charge person.

Making the Choice

When you were a little kid, you probably didn't long for—or even imagine—a career in sales. Ask some local elementary school kids what they want to be when they grow up. You'll find more future firefighters than prospective salespeople. How many children are anxiously anticipating a career of cold-calling, rejection handling, dealing with price-sensitive procurement officers, coping with de-layed flights in center seats, and spending ninety nights a year sleeping in different hotel rooms all next to the same ice machine?

For some of us, it just sort of worked out that way.

You may have "ended up" in sales as a second or third choice when something else didn't work out. You may still be wondering if a career in sales is right for you.

Whether you are an engineer or shop foreman, CEO or account executive, your job increasingly requires excellent sales skills. When I told my neighbor, a prominent veterinarian, I was writing a book called *The Accidental Salesperson*, he said, "I'll buy a copy." No mat-ter how you got into sales, this book is going to show you how to sell on purpose. It will guide you through the entire selling process and show you how to move your prospects through that process without skipping any steps.

It takes an accidental salesperson to know one. I was an acci-dental salesperson just like you. Sales, it seems, is the final frontier for liberal arts graduates who have learned how to learn but don't know how to *do* much else.

As a 1972 graduate with a B.A. in political science, I had three ways to use my degree and maximize the investment my parents had made in my education. I could go to law school, take a job in a politician's office, or become a journalist and cover the political scene.

Although my grades in school had always been great, my score on the Law School Admission Test (LSAT) was the lowest on any standardized test I had ever taken. The score barely would have qualified me to attend an unaccredited night school. I took that as a signal that law probably wasn't right for me.

After graduation, I landed a job as a summer intern for my congressman. There I was, two weeks out of college and working on Capitol Hill in the Cannon House Office Building. But instead of catching "Potomac Fever," I was appalled by the political process as it is played out in real life. The pace is agonizingly slow, and bills become laws by a series of compromises and political favors.

Having eliminated law school and a political career within six weeks of graduating, I decided to pursue that career in journalism. Reporting on the political process I so despised seemed like a good career. I would become the next Walter Cronkite.

At the end of my internship, I returned to my parents' home and began my job search. Since Newark, Ohio, did not have a television station and I didn't have any money to move to a big city, I figured I would start my journalism career by landing a job in the news department at the local radio station. Then, after establishing myself in the business, it would be a fairly simple thing to move to Columbus, Ohio, and be a TV reporter. That would lead to local anchor on the ten o'clock news and then to the network level.

There was only one thing standing in the way of that master plan. The general manager at the local radio station announced during my first interview that he already had two newsmen.

"Chris," he said, "I could put you on as an advertising salesman."

"But you don't understand, Mr. Pricer," I said. "I'm a political science major."

"Chris, my offer still stands."

My inner dialogue went this way: "I'll do anything to get into broadcasting—even sell." My reasoning was that once I was in the door, I could work my way into the news department.

"I'll take it," I said.

It took two weeks for me to disabuse myself of the notion that working my way into news was a good plan. The sales manager left every afternoon around four. The news director worked some nights until eleven, covering the city council meetings. The sales manager drove a Cadillac. The news director drove a beat-up Chevy Vega and constantly bemoaned his fate and income. He often berated the salespeople for making too much money. From an income and status standpoint, I learned quickly that you don't "work your way into news" in a small-market radio station.

At that point, I made "The Choice" to stay in sales. I purchased books on the subject. I attended fantastic seminars and devoured audiocassettes and later CDs on success and selling. I studied selling as hard as I'd studied political science, and it paid off. That choice led to a successful sales career, a promotion to sales management, and radio station ownership in my mid-twenties. In 1983, I founded a company to train radio advertising salespeople. With the publication of *The Accidental Salesperson* in 2000, CEOs, VPs of sales, and owners of family businesses started calling me. All of a sudden, I was doing sales training for start-ups, software companies, manufacturers, and Fortune 500 companies.

Nearly forty years after strolling into that radio station to get a news job, I have conducted more than 2,100 live seminars and keynote speeches; developed dozens of correspondence/distance-learning courses; and created an online-coached and time-released training program based on many of the principles in this book.

Today, I am in what my wife, Sarah, calls "speaker semi-retirement." I work with a few select clients. I am more likely to do thirteen presentations a year rather than the thirteen a month I used to do. But every Monday morning, I turn out a new Knowledge Bite, a digestible three- to seven-minute MP3 file that I upload to my Fuel website, and salespeople worldwide download it. You can get a sample at www.sparquefuel.com.

I was always frustrated with the start-and-stop nature of training programs. Business stopped for a day or two, everyone came to a hotel ballroom and "got trained," and then they went back to work. Some people implemented the training. Others didn't. But I've found that time-releasing training in small bites gains more traction. The idea of continual improvement was a hit in the manufacturing sector, thanks to W. Edwards Deming and others. Today, you can have continual salesperson improvement.

Making "The Choice" to stay in sales and become good at it worked well for me. Choosing to read this book and commit to improving yourself and, therefore, your sales will, I suspect, work just as well for you.

But you know what? Even if I had ended up in law school, I still would be in sales. In a law firm, a "rainmaker" is the attorney who brings clients into the firm. An attorney who can sell is also called a partner.

One day, when I was skiing with a friend who is a dentist, I asked him, "What is the biggest issue in dentistry today?"

"Sales," he replied. "You've got to close people on having their wisdom teeth out. You have to handle objections. You have to persuade and convince them to put up with pain, expense, and time away from work. They don't teach you sales at dental school, but they should."

He made the choice to become a dentist and ended up an accidental salesperson.

So you see, you are not alone. A lot of accidental salespeople have learned to sell on purpose. But first, they have had to make "The Choice."

You do, too.

You make The Choice when you consciously commit to your career in selling. In doing so, you gain a sense of purpose. Being able to say, "This is what I do," and say it with pride and certainty, sets in motion undreamed-of opportunities for success. Choosing to focus on becoming an excellent salesperson is liberating precisely because it eliminates other options you are free to pursue, sometimes to your detriment.

You can experience much the same feeling of liberation tonight by choosing to turn off the TV instead of flipping through channels to find something worth devoting your time to. Or, if you must watch TV, focus on one show to the exclusion of all the others, and take comfort in knowing that you've made the right choice and don't need to zip through the channels so you won't miss anything.

By not focusing, you miss everything.

That's The Choice.

Making the Commitment

Is sales right for you? "Hey, I was looking for a job when I found this one" is the mantra of millions of uncommitted workers today. When you make The Choice consciously and commit to your sales career, you gain a new sense of purpose. Adding that focus makes what you do more relevant.

Developing an obsession with doing things better is vital to success. Until you choose to do it better, no book, audio program, webinar, seminar, or personal growth guru can help you—no matter what your career.

Getting into sales accidentally makes it difficult, but certainly not impossible, to sell on purpose. Therefore, a crucial but simplistic step is to make some purposeful commitments:

- Make a commitment to yourself to succeed.
- Make a commitment to the company you represent.
- Make a commitment to your product or service.
- Make a commitment to your customers.
- Make a commitment to "do it better."

Bringing Good Ideas to the Table

An axiom is a self-evident truth. It requires no proof because it is so obvious. If you buy the axiom below, you are on your way to a fulfilling and rewarding sales career.

A corollary is something that naturally flows from the axiom and therefore incidentally or naturally accompanies or parallels it. Imagine that the corollary starts with the phrase, "It follows that . . ."

Accidental Salesperson Axiom:
Your clients get better when *you* get better.

Corollary:
Your clients are praying for you to get better. They want to work at
the highest levels with the best salespeople in the business.

You can master all of the sales skills and have abundant product knowledge and industry experience, but you will sell even better when you have good ideas to bring to the table. Ideas that make your client's business better make you a better salesperson. Let me explain.

One night after dinner, my friend Tom and I were reminiscing about our sales careers. Tom started his career as a wine salesperson. He called on grocery store managers trying to get them to stock cases of his company's products.

Tom told me a story about one particular store manager who had agreed to purchase two cases of a Sangria-like summer wine. "My goal was to sell him 100 cases," Tom said. As Tom explained, it was a cold day in early spring, and while on his way to meet this manager at the store, he passed a boat dealer putting up a sign advertising preseason prices. This chance occurrence gave Tom an idea.

"You know what you ought to do?" Tom said to the grocery manager. "You ought to get a boat and put it at the front of your store so that people see it when they come in. Then we can fill the boat with cases of the wine to make the tie-in with boating and summer. It will really grab people's attention, and it should be a great way to merchandise this wine."

"Where am I going to get a boat?" the manager asked.

"Let me worry about that," Tom responded.

Tom then drove back to the boat dealer and introduced himself.

"How's business?" he asked.

"Pretty slow. There's still snow on the ground. Nobody is thinking about boating yet."

"You know what might help," Tom said. "You could put one of your boats in the grocery store about a mile from here. Thousands of people would pass by it and see the name of your business right before the season starts."

"How am I going to get the grocery store to let me put a boat in there?" the boat dealer asked.

"You leave that to me," Tom told him. "Could you trailer a boat to the store and get it set up inside?"

"I can trailer and set up a boat anywhere," the boat dealer replied.

Tom went back to the grocery store to tell the manager he had a boat, and as a result of his ingenuity, the store ended up purchasing and selling hundreds of cases of the wine.

Tom's idea solved three problems: (1) his problem of selling his wine, (2) the grocery store owner's problem turning his inventory, and (3) the boat dealer's problem of building traffic in a slow season. Like a chess master, Tom was thinking several moves ahead. He was thinking about how the grocery store could sell more wine to its customers, not just how he could sell some wine to the grocery store. By coming up with an exciting merchandising idea, he made it easy for the store manager to stock up on his product.

You can view yourself as a salesperson with some price sheets and spec sheets. Or you can see yourself as the eyes and ears of your prospects and customers, bringing them news about what's going on out there in the marketplace. After all, you have the advantage of seeing different businesses and different applications of your products and services. You become what sales trainer Jeff Thull calls a "source of business advantage" because of the ideas you bring to the table, not just because of what you are selling.

Paying the Price

Okay, you've made The Choice. You are ready to embark on your own personal sales boom. Let's get something straight, though. If you are going to rise to the top of any profession, you are going to have to pay some kind of price. Imagine putting in four years of college, four years of medical school, and then four years of residency at a hospital where you're on duty for twenty-four hours at a time just to become a physician.

It's called delayed gratification.

Delayed gratification means sacrificing now in anticipation of a bigger reward at some future date. Not only do doctors put in twelve years of intense study and work, they take out massive loans to pay for the privilege.

You got into sales for free. But somewhere along the way you are going to have to pay the price in the form of study, hard work, and long hours. Albert Pujols inks a $240 million contract. Rory McIlory wins the U.S. Open and the prize money, exemptions, and endorsements that revolve around that championship. What you *don't* see is all the work they did for free before they got paid for it. All these "overpaid" pros spent years on the practice field or range in elementary school, junior high, high school, and college getting good enough finally to be paid.

If you are going to make an above-average income in sales, you have to be willing to put in an enormous amount of time and energy (for free) before you are in a position to earn that money.

Sales is hard work, but the rewards for many top salespeople are well worth it. Before you commit to the hard work, you must answer a very important question:

Do you need to be **wanted** or
do you **want** to be **needed**?

Part of the price you pay in selling is dealing with rejection. When you sell on purpose you will start to recognize that most of what you used to call rejection is merely indifference. Still, it is easier to sell things people want to buy than it is to sell things people need but don't necessarily want to buy.

As an outside salesperson, you do a lot more work than a retail clerk. A customer who walks into a clothing store looking for a blue, double-breasted suit is already predisposed to buy. Sure, the salesperson can mess up the sale by not knowing the product, not having your size, or not being attentive. But contrast this in-store situation to a scenario in which the salesperson in the blue, double-breasted suit is calling on a buyer and trying to discover a need for a new product or process. This salesperson has to sell the first meeting, sell the second meeting, and sell the client on investing enough time to determine if there is a need. Then the salesperson must persuade the prospect there is a need and develop a sense of urgency so that the prospect acts. The salesperson does this by creating a vision of a more efficient and profitable operation and offering evidence that purchasing the product will result in the vision.

There is one opportunity after another to fail. Clients reject your approaches and hide from your phone calls.

That's why outside salespeople earn more money than retail clerks.

Then there are your well-meaning parents, friends, and spouse.

They question how you can take the rejection and uncertainty of selling. One of my friends once told me that he didn't understand how I could go to work not knowing how much money I was going to bring home at the end of the month. "That's a lot of pressure," he said.

I thought to myself, "I'd rather not know how much I'm going to make this month than be sure about how little I'm going to make. I'd rather have a job where I can get rewarded for productivity and not just get a cost-of-living adjustment at the end of the year."

Working on commission or some kind of salary bonus arrangement gives you the tremendous opportunity to give yourself a monthly merit increase. That's the good news.

Your clients also want you to get better, but they are not always encouraging. You may get all excited about "doing it better" one day and be looking at the want ads at lunch because a client rejected you. It's going to take some time.

If you want to be needed, you must persist despite the resistance. You must make your clients' lives better and their businesses more profitable. Then something wonderful happens: Your clients give you referrals and your prospects promptly return your calls.

At that point, you are wanted because clients realize how much they need your expertise. You have become a partner instead of a vendor.

Sales is a series of defeats punctuated by profitable victories. If you focus on the defeats instead of the victories, you can easily lose sight of your goals. If you understand that you are paying your dues and that it does get better, you will hang in long enough to enjoy better and more profitable relationships.

Becoming a Lifelong Learner

Accidental salespeople don't have a philosophy of sales. Why should they? They are still deciding if they like sales. They doubt selling and themselves. It's hard to develop a philosophy "on the fly." All of a sudden you're in sales. You patch together a sales style that's usually based on salespeople you've met, or as an opposite reaction to stereotypical salespeople you've seen in movies and on television.

A philosophy is a theory underlying or regarding a sphere of activity or thought. Let's start working on your philosophy of selling right now. First, let me share with you my philosophy of selling. I've come to firmly believe that . . .

Life is one big seminar, and lifelong learners get more out of life.

One day a brochure crossed my desk. The headline caught my eye. It read, HOW TO WRITE BROCHURES THAT SELL. The brochure advertised a six-hour seminar. The cost of the seminar seemed reasonable. I wanted to learn more about writing brochures that sell. So you know what I did?

You guessed it. I studied the brochure for three hours and incorporated all the ideas I found into my brochure. Hey, if you were trying to sell a seminar on how to write brochures, wouldn't you take your own advice when you produced the brochure? So why invest $129?

Now think about this. I've sold sales training for the past thirty years. When I call on a prospect there is an interesting dynamic at work. He is getting a free sales clinic. I practice what I preach. He is taking in my presentation and also deciding if he wants his salespeople selling to their customers the way I sell to him.

There are sales trainers who teach tactics your gut tells you are wrong. Trust your gut. Unless you are selling time-share condominiums in Mazatlán or fake Rolex watches on the streets of New York City, avoid anything that feels funny or seems tricky. If you want repeat business and referrals, trust and truth will trump tactics.

Professional buyers go to seminars that teach them how to spot salespeople who are using manipulative tactics. As a buyer, there is nothing worse than sitting down with a salesperson who is mechanically mouthing a technique that feels foreign to him.

Imagine that you are in a car dealership and the salesperson looks you in the eye and says, "If you were my own mother, I would suggest that you buy this car today. It's that good a deal."

The salesperson wants you to think to yourself, "I guess this is a really good deal." What you're really thinking is, "What kind of a sucker does this guy take me for? I bet he says that to all his customers."

I wouldn't use a tactic like that on my own mother. I don't teach them, either.

Just as I learned lessons on how to write brochures from the brochure I received, you can learn as much from a tough customer as you can from a professor or professional speaker. Some of the best sales seminars I've ever attended were free. In fact, they weren't even billed as seminars. They just turned out that way. They were "accidental seminars." They were powerful nonetheless.

In each chapter of *The Accidental Salesperson*, I'll tell you a story of an ordinary salesperson giving an extraordinary clinic on how to sell or about a client who taught me how to sell.

ACCIDENTAL SALES TRAINING SEMINAR

The Shoeshine Guy

I am walking through Terminal 2 at Chicago O'Hare International Airport, lugging two heavy bags. I see the shoeshine stand directly ahead. The shoeshine man is looking for his next sale.

I'm walking and thinking about getting to my connecting gate. Somehow he catches my eye. When he has it, he looks down at my shoes. My eyes follow his. As I pass, trying not to look him in the eye again, he says, "Sir, let me shine those Cole Haan loafers for you."

"Uh, no thanks, I've got to catch a plane," I reply. (Now there's an original objection he's never heard before.)

> I keep walking, but now I'm thinking, *How did he know these are Cole Haan shoes? That was an interesting approach. I wonder if they are Cole Haan shoes?*
>
> I duck into the nearest men's room and, balancing on my left foot, I take off my right shoe to read the label. It reads "Cole Haan," and I put it back on and return to the shoeshine stand.
>
> "I've changed my mind. I need a shine, after all."

Are you willing to learn from someone who is not a trainer or teacher? This shoeshine professional sold me a $5 shoeshine and threw in seven sales success principles absolutely free. Sure, his service isn't very complex and his sales process isn't nearly as complicated as yours. At the same time, you can benefit from and form a philosophy around these seven ideas:

1. *A strong opening is critical.* When you pass the "typical" shoeshine man, he says, "Shine 'em up?" My pro had taken his approach to a higher level with a customized opening line for each customer. This shoeshine man's opening question and confirmation question are one and the same. Strong opening leads to strong closing.

2. *Product involvement is a powerful success trait.* By calling out the brand of shoe, he was communicating, "Hey, this is what I do. I care about shoes." Wouldn't you rather buy anything from a salesperson who is into what he's doing?

3. *Controlling the focus of the meeting is critical.* The salesperson broke my preoccupation with catching a plane and forced me to focus on my shoes. When you control the focus, you gain more control of the situation. He shifted the focus from getting to my gate to getting my shoes shined.

4. *Eye contact is an important trust-building tool.* You convey confidence with eye contact. Look customers in the eye

and smile with your eyes and mouth. This practice helps to build trust and reduces reluctance to doing business with you.

5. *Helping customers discover needs is part of the process.* By getting me to look down at my shoes, the shoeshine guy allowed me to discover for myself that it had been a while since my shoes had a shiny finish on them. People rarely resist their own data and discoveries.

6. *Doing it differently is refreshing and memorable for the customer.* I have passed thousands of shoeshine stands and had hundreds of shoeshines. I still remember the shoeshine guy who did it a little differently. Will your customers remember you?

7. *Customers buy from salespeople who align their behavior with the things that customers value.* Customers want to buy things. They want to work with professionals. They want to be engaged and challenged.

Because I believe life is one big seminar, and lifelong learners get more out of life, I can get a $129 seminar out of a $0.50 brochure, and I can get seven key selling strategies from a $5 shoeshine (plus tip).

Ralph Waldo Emerson wrote, "Life is a succession of lessons, which must be lived to be understood."

On his way to make that sales call on a grocery store manager, my friend Tom passed a boat dealer who had nobody on his lot; by simply noting that the boat dealer could use some business, Tom parlayed his observation into a huge sale. Keep your eyes and ears open. Ideas are everywhere.

What lessons will you learn today? Who will your teachers be? You never know. Just be open to learning from everyone.

* * *

I am not a motivational speaker. Salespeople leave my seminars with a clear understanding of specific steps they can take to succeed. This "job clarity" can be very motivating. You'll experience it when you finish this book and start to implement the strategies I suggest.

This book will not motivate you to become successful; it will help you be more successful so that you will become motivated. That's the "secret" of motivation most motivational speakers don't speak about.

Achievement is motivating. Closing a sale can boost your enthusiasm.

Look around at the successful people you know who can afford to retire. Few of them do. They are looking for the next challenge and the next achievement.

Life is too short to demand anything less than the best from yourself and to give anything less than your best to your customers. And being the best is a choice you can make today. Choose and you set yourself apart. You'll approach your job and your customers with a renewed sense of interest and purpose. You'll set in motion a chain of events that changes everything for the better. You can do it. You can align yourself with things that buyers value.

It's no accident that you picked up this book. It was a choice. Every day, you make choices about exactly the kind of salesperson you are going to be. Making conscious choices will set you apart from your competitors.

CHAPTER 2

Using the Chart

"Ladies and gentlemen, we've got to take it to the next level."

In well-produced sales meetings at lavish resorts, CEOs and sales managers urge their teams to "take it to the next level."

There is one major problem with these exhortations. Most of us interpret those words to mean, "I've got to work even harder and sell even more than I did last year." Hey, you are already working harder, smarter, and longer than you ever imagined you would. So hearing that you have to take it to the next level is not very motivating, is it?

"Taking it to the next level" is just a bad business cliché unless you have a clear picture of precisely what level you've already attained and are able to envision exactly what the next level will look like when you get there.

That's what we're going to do in this chapter.

When you choose to operate at a higher level, you leverage every prospect contact. It is possible to increase your sales dramatically. It requires no more effort than you are exerting right now, just a different kind of effort. The same territory and the same number of presentations you made last week can yield huge sales increases if you consciously change your selling style.

The far-left column of Figure 2-1 describes various attributes of the selling process. The row across the top indicates the levels of professionalism you have achieved if you exhibit the behaviors in the columns immediately below Level 1, Level 2, and so on. For example, you e-mail a product brochure to a prospect. That's Level 1: Your "presentation" consists of "product literature, spec sheets, rate sheets." On the other hand, if you e-mail a link to an article you've found on golf course maintenance to a customer who sells turf pesticide products, your "approach and involvement" is to be a "true source of industry information and "business intelligence." With that customer, and with that action, you are at Level 3. You are having a "Level 3 moment." And if you have dozens of Level 3 moments every week, you will outshine your competition in the eyes of your customers. There is a powerful cumulative impact that builds up when you actually do take your approach to a higher level.

The Chart adds a component to sales and sales training long missing: the quality component. Immediately, you can begin to apply quality standards and not just quantity standards to your sales process.

As you study The Chart, think about specific customers and prospects. Right away, you'll be able to see what level you have attained with that specific person and envision exactly what the next level is going to look like when you get there.

The Chart shows you how to work smarter.

When the first edition of *The Accidental Salesperson* was published, I was teaching a leadership program and telling my audiences that there were Level 1, 2, 3, and 4 salespeople. Since I wrote the book and knew everything about selling, I glibly rated myself Level 4.

Then something happened. (Something always happens, but not everyone is open to the lessons that that something brings.) A meeting planner called and got through to me instead of our marketing person. "I hear you wrote a book on selling," the caller said, "and my client is thinking about bringing you in to speak at their annual sales meeting."

"What kind of change is the client looking for?" I asked, trying to probe. "How do they want their salespeople to be different or better as a result of my presentation?" (Level 2, at least, was my initial thought.)

Figure 2-1 The Chart can take your career to the next level.

	Level 1 Account Executive	Level 2 Salesperson or Problem Solver	Level 3 Professional Salesperson	Level 4 Sales and Marketing Professional
Level of trust	Neutral or distrustful	Some credibility	Credible to highly credible; based on salesperson's history	Complete trust based on established relationships and past performance
Goal/call objective	To open doors; to "see what's going on"	To persuade and make a sale or to advance the project through the process	Customer creation and retention; to "find the fit"; to upgrade the client and gain more information	To continue upgrading and increase share of business
Approach and involvement	Minimal ot nonexistent	Well-planned; work to get prospect to buy into the process	True source of industry information and "business" intelligence"	Less formal and more comfortable because of trust and history
Concern or self-esteem issue	Being liked	Being of service; solving a problem	Being a resource	Being an "outsider insider"
Precall preparation	Memorize a canned pitch or "wing it"	Sell call objectives; prescript questions; articulate purpose-process-payoff	Research trade magazines; Internet; analyze client's competition	Thorough preparation sometimes with proprietary information unavailable to other reps
Presentation	Product literature, spec sheets, rate sheets	Product solution for problem they uncover during need analysis	Systems solutions	Return on investment proof and profit investment strategies
Point of contact	Buyer or purchasing agent	End users as well as buyer or purchasing agent	Buyers, end users, and an "internal coach" or advocate within client's company	"Networked" through the company; may be doing business in multiple divisions

DEFAULT   Preference settings

The answer I got was, "Look, Chris, I'm the meeting planner. I'm going to look at seven videos and seven fee structures and pick a speaker. Do you want to play or not?"

"Sure, I'll play."

"Then send me a video and your fees."

As I directed our assistant to package and send a video to the meeting planner, I realized that all I was doing was sending Level 1 information.

And I wrote the book!

A veteran salesperson can have a Level 1 conversation in the morning—just like I did—and a Level 4 meeting in the afternoon. I have come to think of The Chart as a relationship analyzer or a meeting evaluator that allows both you (and me) to see exactly how strong or weak our relationships are.

As bestselling author and leadership development architect Susan Scott so aptly put it in her book, *Fierce Conversations: Achieving Success at Work and in Life, One Conversation at a Time*, "Your last conversation is the relationship." That is true because your prospects and customers are besieged by phone calls, e-mails, and meetings and don't have time to think much about the meeting they just had with you once you walk out of their offices.

If you approach them at Level 1, they will lump you with all the other product-pushing, price-sheet-wielding salespeople who don't add value by their presence.

There's one more thing about The Chart, and it's a very important one. You can approach a prospect at Level 2 instead of Level 1 and that's a 100 percent improvement. Don't worry about getting to Level 3 or Level 4 at first. In fact, you really don't have a business relationship until somebody writes you a check. Only when you've solved a business problem for a customer and spent some time on the account can you continually develop the relationship and take it to the next level.

Only now you know exactly what that next level looks like.

The Chart is like a GPS system that tells you where you are with the customer and where you need to go.

What Kind of Salesperson Will You Choose to Be?

In a *New York Times* theater review, Walter Goodman once wrote this about Arthur Miller's *Death of a Salesman*: "Whether the attention comes from academics or journalists or a playwright or two, the salesman is most commonly a figure of mockery, particularly if he is a traveling man.... The calling is seldom held up as an exemplar of high aspirations or edifying values."

The messages that the media put into our brains about selling conspire to defeat accidental salespeople before they even begin to discover what selling on purpose is all about.

As an accidental salesperson, you have to confront and vanquish the stigma of selling. The Chart helps you do that. Since Arthur Miller penned *Death of a Salesman*, most media portrayals of salespeople have been negative. Miller's character Willy Loman was deeply flawed. The salespeople in David Mamet's *Glengarry Glen Ross* used high-pressure tactics and wallowed in low self-esteem. I'll have to confess that even I have kept the lights off and hidden in a back room of my house when someone knocked on my door. I always assume it's someone soliciting funds for a cause or selling a particular brand of religion. And occasionally it's a local politician asking for votes. It's almost the same kind of fear that Pee-wee Herman feigned when the door-to-door salesman rang the bell of the Playhouse. "Saaaalesmaaan!" he screamed as he ran from the door. (Just for fun, go to YouTube and search for Pee-wee Herman-SALESMAN! And enjoy the silliness.)

You didn't get into sales to frighten people. In fact, most accidental salespeople chose their selling style in order not to be perceived as a typical salesperson.

Early sales training was essentially a boot camp for professional stalkers. A stalker is a person who persists despite the wishes of another person. Today there are laws to prevent stalking.

In the early days, sales techniques and sales pressure took precedence over solving a prospect's problem. Sales, as it was taught a few decades ago and is portrayed in the media, is a stressful way to make a living. I recall listening to an early sales training record; the speaker was J. Douglas Edwards. I visualized him pacing the platform in front of a packed auditorium as he exhorted the salespeople in the audience.

"Gentlemen," he said, "when you ask a closing question, shut up. Shut . . . up! Because the next person who talks"—and he paused—"*loses*." (This was before women started getting into and excelling at sales.)

That ancient piece of advice has been passed down through several generations of salespeople. It is on the lips of even the newest salespeople, however.

Think about the implications of that mindset. If you believe you are selling something that only losers buy, you will take a hit to your self-esteem even when you make a sale. While the "silence close" is legitimate, the idea that someone has to lose in order to do business with us is flawed.

As Strother Martin's character told Paul Newman's character in the movie *Cool Hand Luke*, "You've got to get your mind right."

To get your mind right, you have to have a different picture of what "good" looks like in selling. It is vital to replace the stereotypical salesperson who stigmatizes the profession with a vision of yourself operating at Level 2 or higher on The Chart.

In computer-speak, the option the system or software chooses when you don't indicate a choice yourself is called the default mode. If you don't tell Microsoft Word your font and type size "preferences," Bill Gates has already set the software's "default" at 12-point Times New Roman.

Too often, accidental salespeople choose a selling style as a re-action to the negative stereotypes. If being pushy is bad, then being more passive must be better. Accidental salespeople often default to Level 1. Many salespeople never grasp that, in sales, the opposite of pushy isn't passive, but professionally persistent.

The Chart helps you make The Choice of what kind of salesperson you are going to be. Level 1 is the default mode. Unfortunately, it's where many people who ended up in sales end up.

"I was in the neighborhood and thought I'd pop in to see if you needed anything" is a Level 1 approach.

Putting together a packet of product literature to take to the first meeting with the client is a Level 1 behavior.

"Anything coming down for me this week?" is a Level 1 question.

E-mailing price lists and product literature is a Level 1 activity.

As you look at The Chart, you may see that you have some clients with whom you are operating at Level 1. You may be operating at Level 2 or higher with other clients. You take your career to the next level by taking your relationship with *each client* to the next level.

Obviously, reacting to client requests is sometimes necessary. Just know that when you are being reactive, you're at Level 1. Some clients may even demand Level 1 behavior because they don't know any better. It is your job to override their default mode and begin setting your own preferences. I call this "selling customers on the way you sell."

Selling on Purpose

Making a conscious choice to operate at Level 2 or higher is how an accidental salesperson starts to sell on purpose.

Think of Level 2 as the "base camp" from which to launch your assault on the summit of sales professionalism. Mountain climbers establish base camp partway up the mountain. They don't start their climb from the valley.

Look at The Chart to see how trust evolves. Level 4 salespeople have complete trust based on established relationships and past performance. That may take ten years. You cannot wait ten years.

Fortunately, you can get to Level 2 very early in your career. Set your preference at Level 2 and your clients will perceive you as 100 percent better than every Level 1 salesperson who approaches them—since most salespeople *are* Level 1 salespeople. Next, choose to have several Level 3 or Level 4 "moments" with your prospects and clients every week.

Have you ever sent a link to an article about an issue or trend in the prospect's industry to that prospect in an e-mail? If you have, you had a Level 3 "moment." You chose to be a source of industry information and business intelligence. (You weren't necessarily at Level 3 all day, though, or with every other prospect.) You can also put Level 3 and 4 "pages" in your presentations. (More on that idea later.)

These Level 3 moments add up. They have a profound effect on your prospects and customers. Buyers may not have The Chart on their desks to rate salespeople. However, after seeing a parade of salespeople march through their offices, buyers develop a built-in rating system they apply to each salesperson.

Moving from Level 1 to Level 2 on The Chart means that you are aligning your sales behavior with those things that buyers value most in salespeople. That will make you a tough act for a competitor to follow. Prospects and clients are like Olympic figure skating judges. They rate salespeople who call on them—and there aren't many perfect scores. Here is part of a letter from a client to a sales manager who had enrolled a salesperson in one of our programs:

> Dear Kelly,
>
> I am writing to tell you about the kind of service that I am getting from your sales associate, Kim Delwiche. Kim has taken our account, educated us about your services, and offered us solid information and evidence to back up her suggestions. If you don't have a nickname for Kim, may I suggest "The Yardstick"? Why "The Yardstick"? She sets the standard by which we measure all of the other salespeople in the marketplace.
>
> Sincerely,
> Ray Lassee, Manager

Imagine you were the salesperson who walked into Ray's office right after Kim. It would be like having to figure skate after Olympic gold medalist Kim Yu-na had just completed her routine. No matter how good you are, you are going to be held to a higher standard by the judges.

Now here's the rest of the story. Kim had only been in her sales position for six months. She distanced herself from the pack without tricks or manipulation. She simply aligned her behavior with the behavior that her prospects and clients value.

You may not have a worldwide audience like Kim Yu-na. Your clients don't pass out gold, silver, and bronze medals. They do, however, evaluate your performance daily and award the better performances with orders.

Do you know why Ray Lassee buys more from Kim than he does from the other representatives who call on him? One of the reasons is that he spends more time with her. You buy time when you gain trust.

Kurt Lewin, often considered the father of social psychology, said, "There is nothing more practical than a good theory." What I would have given to have The Chart to plug into for modeling my process when I started my career in sales.

Learning from Your Clients

Getting a letter from a client (like Kelly's letter on Kim) is one way to know that you're on track. Sometimes the feedback doesn't come in the form of a letter. It comes by the way the client reacts. Life is one big seminar. Lifelong learners get more out of life. Your clients can teach you a lot about selling by the way they react to you.

Here's a story about what one client taught me. First, some background: It was 1976, and I was selling radio advertising in Madison, Wisconsin. I had hair. I had a positive mental attitude. I carried a fiberglass briefcase, wore a leisure suit, and drove an orange AMC Gremlin.

ACCIDENTAL SALES TRAINING SEMINAR

The Car Dealer Who Canceled His Order

In 1976, there were no cell phones, no fax machines, no e-mail. We had a message nail. When you walked into the office, the first thing you did was retrieve all the little pink message slips from the message nail and go through them to see which calls needed to be returned. One afternoon there was a message for me from the new manager at one of my car dealer clients. The fact that the message was written on a pink slip was ironic because, in essence, the new guy was firing me.

The message read: "Bob Voss, Schappe-Conway Dodge, called. Cancel all of our advertising schedules immediately. You will have a twenty-minute meeting to repitch the entire year's advertising budget on Thursday. Your appointment with Mr. Voss is at 1:20 p.m." Twenty minutes to present an entire year's advertising program. The meeting was in forty-eight hours.

The bad news: The client had canceled his advertising. The worse news: I was his 1:20 meeting. That meant he was meeting with sales reps from every media for twenty minutes each. He had an 8:00, 8:20, 8:40, 9:00, 9:20, 9:40, and so on. I was going to be the fourteenth media rep he would see that day.

Mr. Voss canceled his advertising on Tuesday. The twenty-minute meeting was set for Thursday. In preparing for the meeting, I called a salesperson at the dealership. I learned from her that Mr. Voss had just been hired away from Dodge City in Milwaukee to turn around the Dodge dealership in Madison. For those of you who can remember back that far, 1976 was the pre–Lee Iacocca era, and Dodge was struggling nationwide.

I planned my approach.

I decided I didn't want to be like every other rep, in there for twenty minutes desperately presenting the year's budget. My goal was to sell Mr. Voss on the fact that twenty minutes wasn't long enough to plan a year's worth of advertising. My strategy was to differentiate myself and my presentation from that parade of media reps I imagined he was meeting with and the presentations they were making.

I made a conscious decision to not even present him a year's schedule, even though that was what he requested. I left the Arbitron local ratings book at the station. I didn't pack a rate sheet or a brochure on the station. All I had in my fiberglass briefcase when I walked in the door was my customer needs analysis form and a notepad.

At precisely 1:20 p.m. on Thursday, the door of Mr. Voss's office opened and out came the salesperson from the one o'clock meeting. He was rolling his eyes and surreptitiously shaking his head in disgust. As he made his exit, I made my entrance. As I walked into Mr. Voss's office with my briefcase in my left hand, I extended my right hand and said, "Good afternoon, Mr. Voss, I'm Chris L—"

And he said, as gruffly as you can imagine, "You're my 1:20 appointment. Sit down and pitch me." He said it in an obnoxious but not abusive way.

This is going to be an interesting meeting, I thought to myself. I had never been to a seminar on neurolinguistics to learn about mirroring a client, but I was astute enough to realize that here was a tough customer, and I had better change my style of selling and become the salesperson he wanted me to be. Gruff, quick, and to the point. Get to the bottom line.

"Mr. Voss, I don't know if you should be on our station or not," I said. I knew he hadn't heard that line from any one of the thirteen eager salespeople who had come before me.

"What do you mean you don't know if I should be on your station or not?" he shot back.

"Well, Mr. Voss, I know that you're already a successful car dealer, and I've heard about your work with Dodge City. We're having the biggest month in the history of our radio station. So we're both successful and we're doing it without each other."

(Let me add that I was twenty-six years old, and even back then, I wanted to see myself as providing a valuable service instead of taking someone's money.)

I looked him in the eye and said, "I work with Len Mattioli at American TV, Jon Lancaster at his dealership, and the Copps account. I'm helping them get some big sales increases. This is the way I work with them. See if it makes sense to you."

And I continued: "Most of my important clients want ideas that help them improve traffic, sales, and profits. In order to be in a position to bring ideas instead of just rates and ratings, I use a tool that helps me learn about nine key areas of your business that may give you an advertisable difference over your competitors. It takes anywhere from an hour to an hour and one half to do it right.

"I could present a schedule and show you what your predecessor and I were working on. But I imagine you have bigger goals and tougher targets than Steve did, or you wouldn't be in that chair.

"Mr. Voss," I finally said, "I want to be in a position to make an intelligent proposal based on your objectives and not just my need to sell you a schedule. Does that make sense?"

"Yes," he said, his voice softening a little bit.

And then I made The Gesture. I raised my hand and gestured to his credenza and he looked around. On the credenza was the pile of media kits that every other salesperson had brought to the meeting.

"Mr. Voss," I said, still gesturing at the stack, "have you had any intelligent proposals so far today?"

The man changed before my very eyes. The gruff, powerful executive was now slumping in his chair. His face sagged. He looked at me and said these words: "Chris, this has been the most boring day of my life."

"Mr. Voss? Can we go through this analysis together?"

"Chris, please, call me Bob."

"Bob, what are your plans for turning this dealership around?"

Ninety minutes later, Bob Voss accompanied me out of his office. There were four salespeople in the waiting room, like planes circling over O'Hare on a stormy night.

Two weeks later, the client was back on our station in a big way and was one of the top-ten advertisers on the station that year.

The most boring day of Bob Voss's life was made up of thirteen consecutive Level 1 presentations. Level 1 selling bores clients, even if that's what they ask for. Because I approached him at Level 2, every other salesperson became an easy act to follow.

I might have made a quicker sale if I had pitched him in the allotted twenty minutes, but I don't think I would have made a bigger or longer-lasting sale. I would have been just one of the vendors he bought from, not one of the people he looked to for advertising advice and ideas.

And it doesn't matter what you're selling.

I got six lessons from that accidental seminar. Here they are:

1. *Tough customers don't want to deal with pushover salespeople.* By being as tough as Bob (in a polite way), I was able to win his respect. And I also didn't take it personally. "Sit down and pitch me, you're my 1:20 appointment." You know what? He probably said that to all of the salespeople who showed up at 8:00, 8:20, and so on. The only difference was that I didn't pitch him on the station. I pitched him on giving me more time. I pitched him on the way I sold instead of what I was trying to sell.

2. *You've got to be different.* Doing it differently doesn't always mean doing it better. But too many salespeople walk in to see what's going to happen and not to make something happen. The result is a bored client. It still amazes me that someone could meet with thirteen advertising reps and call it the most boring day of his life. In sales, having an interesting approach or a different approach is vital. But you'll never get there without learning the next lesson . . .

3. *Precall planning is vital.* I believe it's a must-have skill, and in Chapter 8 you'll get my precall planning checklist. If you have a meeting tomorrow, skip ahead and preplan it now. I will tell you this: If I hadn't preplanned the call and thought about exactly what I wanted to get out of it, I wouldn't have been able to pull it off. But because I had a plan and clear objectives, I didn't get sucked into the vortex of having to pitch an annual contract in twenty minutes. I was clear about what I wanted from the call and able to get it.

4. *The customer is always right, unless the customer is wrong.* But you can't come right out and tell him he's wrong. Bob Voss was buying advertising the way some of his customers were buying cars. "Give me your best deal. There are lots of competitors. If you don't have what I need, I'm going to go elsewhere," blah-blah-blah. But by taking some time to establish my own credibility and power, I was able to sell him on a better way to buy advertising.

5. *You've got to be willing to walk away from a bad deal or a bad character.* "We're having the biggest month in our station's history, and you're already a success," I said, "and we're doing it without each other." I wanted his business, but I didn't need his business. Approaching the client as an equal and not as a subordinate is a very difficult thing to do for young sellers and people with low self-esteem. You've got to take a tremendous amount of belief into every call—the belief that you can deliver a product or service that is of more value than the money the client is investing with you.

6. *Have friends inside the organization.* I always made it a practice to talk to the car salespeople and the office staff and the service guys so that when the new manager came I could learn a little bit about him before I went to see him for the first time.

The behavior I described in the Bob Voss story resulted in a large, long-term piece of business. But if I had needed to be wanted, I wouldn't have talked to the prospect the way I did. I wanted to be needed—and that made all the difference.

Accidental Salesperson Axiom:
You can't bore people into buying.

Corollary:
Your clients buy the way you sell before they buy what you sell.

Communicating the Way You Work

The sooner you sell prospects on how you are going to work together, the faster they will buy your product. This is the simplistic but profound concept that allows you to break through barriers that buyers build between you and their checkbooks. And it brings us to what I call the magic phrase:

Magic Phrase

"This is the way I work...."

When you utter those words, you communicate to the prospect that you have an organized, planned approach to sales and to solving the problem. Understanding that sales is a process, and being able to articulate the steps in your process, separates you from the pack and positions you as a professional.

If you cannot sell the client on your sales process, you are going to have a tough time selling the client your product or service. Too many salespeople try to take shortcuts. If you try to sell your product before going through the process, you are going to get a lot more objections.

Bob Voss bought *the way* I sold that day. Two weeks later, he started buying a lot of *what* I sold. It is much easier for the prospect to buy the way you sell. It doesn't cost anything but a little time. Your product, on the other hand, costs money.

The strategy is simple: Starting with your next meeting, tell your prospects how you are going to sell to them before you try to sell them your product or service. There is tremendous power in the approach. Skipping this one simple step is very common and very costly to salespeople.

Accidental Salesperson Axiom:

Your strategy is to reveal your strategy.

Corollary:

When clients know what's going to happen, they can quit defending against your tactics and start participating in the process.

The first step, then, is selling your prospect on the way you sell. You tell the client exactly what is going to happen and when it's going to happen. Once you say the magic phrase and articulate your strategy, the air is clear, the atmosphere set. Clients don't have to guard against your tactics, because they already know what is going to happen. If your selling process requires three meetings, you say so. You indicate that the third meeting is when you'll make your presentation and ask for an order. That frees your client from having to mount a defensive response. There are no tactics to guard against.

The minute you use this strategy you'll gain an advantage over your competitors because the buyer's defensive stance is nonexistent. It isn't that you've performed a trick to remove natural defenses when you use the strategy; a defensive attitude never develops in the first place.

You already know you should spend more of your selling time listening than talking. When you tell your customers how you work and what you intend to do, you are psychologically available to listen. When you meet with a client for the first time, you aren't looking for an opportunity to slip in a line or two about how great your product is or how bad your competitor's product performs. You no longer feel the internal pressure to hurry the process along in order to quickly get to the point where you can use a closing technique. You've already sold your client on going through the steps in your selling process with you. Just follow through and back up your words with a sound needs analysis and then present your proposal. Closing becomes the natural outcome of opening the sale properly and going through the steps in your process.

Approaching the prospect properly is the key. Opening the sale takes more finesse than closing. When the client knows how you work, there is less tension and more collaboration. You become a partner instead of a pleader.

I have often asked salespeople how they sell after they have made their quota for the month or quarter. Inevitably, they describe a relaxed approach to the sales process. They slow down and listen to their prospects. They don't feel pressure to sell, so they don't put pressure on their prospects. When I told Bob Voss that we were successful without each other, it elevated me in his eyes.

I didn't need the sale.

How would you sell if you didn't need to make the sale? Would selling like that help you make more sales?

Let me give you an example. When I golfed, I was always an unhappy high handicapper. Then one day I played a nearly flawless front nine while I was on vacation in Michigan. I shot a 39. I had rarely broken 90 in the past, so as Sarah, my wife and partner, and I grabbed a hot dog at the turn, my self-talk was out of control: "I may shoot a 78. I may not only break 90, but I could break 80. All I have to do is keep playing the way I am . . ."

But, of course, I hit seven balls into the water on the back nine and shot a 54 for my typical 93.

In golf, you have to focus on the shot at hand. You can't get too far into the future.

In sales, you have to focus on the content of the customer's conversation and the process—you have to pay attention to how well you are working together. Don't get too far ahead of yourself. Don't be preoccupied with whether you'll close. Focus on the moment you are in and enjoy the process.

The reality is that one sale will not make or break your sales career. You will have to make more sales, whether you make this one or not.

Leaving Your Comfort Zone

Anne Tyler's novel *The Accidental Tourist* inspired the title of this book. The story of a travel writer, Macon, who detests traveling probably resonates with an accidental salesperson who would rather be doing something else.

St. Augustine wrote, "The world is a book, and those who do not travel read but one page." In *The Accidental Tourist*, Macon tries to make every country just like home so that he doesn't have to experience the jarring, disorienting effects of travel. But jet lag, foreign languages, driving on the other side of the road, funny colored currency, and different foods are part of the travel experience. Those things either wake up your senses, causing you to delight in a new way of seeing the world, or they cause you to flee to the familiar.

That's what makes *The Accidental Tourist* a powerful lesson on selling. To succeed, you have to leave your comfort zone, make human contact, and risk the devastating feelings of rejection. You must learn to anticipate and embrace change, instead of struggling to maintain the status quo.

The Roman philosopher Seneca said, "It is not because things are difficult that we do not dare; it is because we do not dare that they are difficult."

Getting into sales accidentally has a similar jarring effect on people. You must overcome much of your early childhood experience to succeed in selling.

"Don't speak to strangers."

"Speak when you're spoken to."

"Don't brag."

And my personal favorite, "Take care." Even at age 61, my mother still tells me to "take care" every time we say good-bye.

"I love you. Take care."

How many times have you heard the words "take care" from your parents and well-meaning friends and flight attendants?

"Bye-bye. Take care."

"Bye now. Take care."

Now think about the number of times you've heard the words "Go for it," or "Take a risk," or "Start your own business. You can do it." Or "You'd make a great salesperson."

What are you going to do today that is uncomfortable but necessary to your own success? You're not a kid anymore, and even in an easy chair, life can find you.

It's your choice.

You've already made The Choice to commit to the sales profession (or at least to keep reading). And now you have The Chart to help you figure out which level of professionalism you've achieved and to help you envision what "the next level" looks like. It would appear that you are ready to meet The Challenge.

CHAPTER 3

Meeting the Challenge

The Challenge is to choose from The Chart the kind of salesperson you are going to be every time you interact with a prospect. The moment you do that, you cease to be an accidental salesperson and start to sell on purpose. The result: instant differentiation.

Since you are competing with other accidental salespeople, your newfound sense of purpose sets you apart. You start to set the standard for how selling is done in your industry.

The Sales "Profession"

There is plenty of debate as to whether sales is a true profession. Merriam-Webster's Collegiate Dictionary defines profession as "a calling requiring specialized knowledge and often long and intensive academic preparation." By that standard, selling is not a profession in the same way that law or medicine is.

Professionals have to meet rigorous standards in order to ply their trade. They generally choose their line of work consciously. They make sacrifices in order to be able to pursue their chosen line of work. There are often rigorous examinations to pass before professionals are allowed to talk to clients. Think about the pressure a newly minted lawyer faces in having to study for and pass the state bar examination.

Even my barber has to have a license to give me a number 2 buzz cut. It's framed and hanging next to the mirror. The sad fact is that most salespeople have fewer hours of training than their barber or hairstylist.

You can certainly approach sales as a profession. You are reading this book, which is a start. You can get the equivalent of an MBA watching college lectures on YouTube and TED. You can set a period of time to work *on* your business instead of *in* your business each week.

Professional firefighters go to an academy to learn how to put out fires and perform lifesaving emergency medical procedures to assist the injured, and then they continue to rigorously train throughout their entire careers. In my seminars, I often quote one of Kurt Russell's lines from *Backdraft*, a movie about firefighters: "You have a bad day here and somebody dies."

What if *you* had a job that required you to have one good day after another or else somebody would die? And that somebody could be you. Do you think you might come to work a little more focused? Would you be a little bit more "into" what you're doing?

Professionalism connotes the idea of continual education and improvement. If you have the desire to learn and to hone your skills, you can strive to be a sales professional.

No Bad Days!

"No bad days" has become a mantra for me. "No bad days" is a very high standard. It is the standard to which we routinely hold the professionals we deal with, whether they are doctors, dentists, or CPAs. A surgeon who has a bad day may be slapped with a malpractice suit as a result. Professionals in many fields are required to have one good day after another.

I challenge you to examine your professionalism using the standard of firefighters, who set higher standards for themselves. It's no accident that many firefighters live to retire after twenty or thirty years of service. Their training and constant retraining prepare them to approach each fire as a professional.

It is possible to have one good day after another in sales, too. But first, you have to believe it's possible. Second, you have to understand that good days are made up of good meetings, and good meetings contain conscious Level 2, 3, and 4 "moments." Having one good day after another is the choice professionals make.

Prediction: The idea of allowing yourself a bad day eventually will become a foreign concept. Of course, this change in mindset means more money for you and your family, but just as important, you'll find more fulfillment and enjoyment in your career. When you sell on purpose and align your behavior with the things that prospects value, you have one good meeting after another. That is how you build one good day after another.

Professional Speakers Are Not Supposed to Have Bad Days, Either

It was an important seminar for a major TV group. There were just twenty people in the room. However, nearly 800 were "attending" via satellite in dozens of other venues.

This was real-time "distance learning." It required only that the speaker travel a great distance. Five minutes before airtime, I walked past the group VP who had hired me.

"Are you ready?" he asked.

I answered with a question of my own: "What are my choices?"

He smiled as if he didn't mind my smart-aleck answer.

There is something wonderful about structure. Having to start and end at a specific time rivets my attention and creates focus.

What are your choices? One of the great things about sales is that for many hours during the day, there is no one watching you. Yet, for too many salespeople, that lack of structure gives them too many choices.

Having high standards for yourself, and holding yourself to those standards, is one way to create structure.

Part of the manager's job is to create structure and systems that cause people to do the right things whether or not they feel like it. It's part of your job, too. That's what pros do. "Management is doing those things necessary to deny people who work for you the unpleasant opportunity of failing." That advice from management consultant Ferdinand F. Fournies is critical for you because only people who sell on purpose will set stringent standards for themselves.

The Three Secrets of Success

"Chris, there are three secrets of success," said my dinner companion. We were finishing our dessert on a flight from Chicago to San Francisco.

I rarely talk with people on airplanes because of the inevitable question they ask: "What do you do for a living?"

"I'm a professional speaker. I don't want to talk about it," I'm always tempted to say. Once people know you are a professional speaker, they have to ask the next question: "What do you speak about?" You can end up giving two or three extra talks a week on airplanes.

This time my dinner companion had initiated the conversation before I even had a chance to put on my headset or bury my nose in a book.

I asked him what he did for a living.

"I'm retired."

Amazed that such a young-looking man could be retired, I asked what he had retired from.

"Chris, I invented a software program that helps businesses track their inventory in multiple locations. We got some venture capitalists to back the company and just went public," he said.

Life is one big seminar. I spent the next hour and a half grilling this guy: "How did you get venture capital? How did you get your product into Fortune 500 companies? Who did you work with to do the IPO?"

I'm sure he got tired of talking to me. Over dessert he said, "Chris, would you like to know the secret of success?"

These are the words I wrote in my diary that night. I didn't write down the name of my teacher, but we were in first class on United, so you can trust the source.

"The first secret of success is that you have to know what you're doing." There are a lot of people who fail simply because they don't study their industry. They don't go to seminars. They don't read. And they fail. However, knowing what you are doing isn't enough.

"The second secret of success is that you have to *know* you know what you're doing." Success is a process, and repeating successful behaviors over and over again is the key. But you have to know what is working so that you can repeat what's working.

"The third secret of success is that you have to be known for what you know." Other people have to know you know what you're doing. When other people know you know what you're doing, they come to you for help and advice, not just for your lowest price.

The Challenge, then, is to choose from The Chart (as presented in Chapter 2) the kind of salesperson you are going to be during every client interaction. And to become known for what you know—and not just about what you sell.

Accidental salespeople do make sales, but they're not exactly sure how they did it. Because they are in a reactive mode most of the day, they don't feel that they have much control over who buys what. To them, sales involves "timing" and "luck."

When you begin to sell on purpose, you immediately separate yourself from the crowd of people who are selling but who don't really want to be. You make conscious daily decisions about what you're going to do and why, in order to take people through your process.

Your clients might even catch some of your increased confidence. But how does the client know you're a pro?

You have made The Choice. You've accepted The Challenge of choosing from The Chart the kind of salesperson you're going to be on every client interaction. You're going to sell on purpose. You have decided to have one good day after another. The next step is communicating this choice to your prospects and customers so that they can differentiate the "new you" from the "old you." At the same time, you want to separate yourself from the pack of salespeople lining the lobbies of your customers' businesses.

You have to market your professionalism to the prospect.

Professionals prepare differently. Golfer Jack Nicklaus famously told John Madden, "I practice after the round. The first thing I practice is all the shots I hit poorly. Then I practice all the shots I didn't have to hit that day." If you have ever banged a bucket of balls and then played eighteen holes, let that statement sink in. Watch *Backdraft* and see how rigorously the firefighters train. Go on vacation with my friend Don, a fifty-eight-year-old 747 captain who is taking his recertification test and see how little skiing and how much studying he does.

You want your customers to trust you. Your personal credibility and trust are vital parts of any successful salesperson-client relationship.

You've got to market your professionalism and not just sell your product.

So many salespeople skip the step of marketing what they know to the prospect. Yet, if they don't skip it, they soon discover they have an immediate point of differentiation. Here's a story that illustrates the essence of marketing professionalism.

ACCIDENTAL SALES TRAINING SEMINAR

Ladies and Gentlemen, This Is Your Captain Speaking . . .

In the early nineties, USAir (now US Airways) had five crashes in five years. Airline travel is extremely safe, with a mortality risk of about one in 40 million. So for one airline to have five crashes in five years is an extreme example of very bad luck, pilot error, mechanical failures, and/or coincidence.

One of USAir's crashes occurred at LaGuardia Airport in New York City. According to published reports, the pilot and copilot had never flown together before. It was a stormy night. As they barreled down the runway, the pilot thought that the copilot had done the preflight checks. The copilot assumed the pilot had done them. Too late they discovered that nobody had done the cockpit checks. The flaps were not set properly, so the airplane could not lift off. As the East River loomed off the end of the runway, an instant decision was made to abort the takeoff. They reversed the engines and put on the brakes. The landing gear collapsed and the plane slid nose up into the East River. Two passengers died and sixty-four were injured.

The Federal Aviation Administration (FAA) investigation revealed that pilot error and not weather was the chief factor in this airline accident. In fact, the headline in *USA Today* two months later read, "Tape reveals USAir crew's mistakes."

Flash-forward three weeks from the USAir crash. I was sitting on an American Airlines flight out of Chicago. I was in the first-class cabin filled with business flyers on their way to their next meeting. The flight attendants did the usual safety announcements.

Then the captain flipped on his microphone and made an announcement. I suspect that he was reading from a script written by the marketing department. If not, he created nonetheless one of the greatest sales pitches for his airline. He said these exact words: "Ladies and gentlemen, this is your captain speaking. We are currently number two for takeoff. I have completed my preflight checklist and would like the flight attendants to please be seated."

The impact of the pilot's new greeting on the frequent flyers in the cabin was immediate and dramatic. My attention perked up and my body involuntarily relaxed. Several seatmates let out a sigh of relief and visibly relaxed. The price of the ticket was the furthest thing from their minds. Any apprehension about flying today was alleviated by the very professional approach of the captain, who told us that he had completed his preflight checklist.

The big lesson: You have to market your professionalism and not just assume that your clients know you're a pro.

Most pilots wouldn't think of taking off without doing their preflight checks. Nor would they think to point out to passengers that they had done it. And yet, something the American Airlines pilot took for granted had a profound impact on his passengers—the airline's customers.

So what do you do behind the scenes that, if your customers knew you had done it, would make them feel more comfortable about doing business with you? You can have a profound effect on your customers by telling them what you do for them when they aren't looking, just like the pilot marketed his professionalism to a cabin full of uptight frequent flyers.

Magic Phrase

"In preparing for this meeting, I . . ."

Today, Airline pilots operate behind closed and locked doors. Similarly, most of the work you do on behalf of your customers happens behind the scenes. Customers do not think about you as much as you think about them. They have many other problems and concerns competing for their attention.

Going the extra mile is fine. *Marketing* the fact that you've gone the extra mile is how you gain extra mileage from your efforts.

The next time you meet with a prospect or customer, open the meeting with this phrase: "In preparing for this meeting, I . . ."

Then quickly list two or three things you did to prepare. You will experience a new level of attention and respect from both clients and prospects. And you'll blow away competitors whose idea of a good sales opening is, "Anything coming down for me this week?" Or, "Your account has just been assigned to me."

If you don't tell them, they'll never know. Remember the big question: What are you doing behind the scenes for your clients that, if your clients knew you were doing it, would make them feel more comfortable about doing business with you? Once you've answered the big question for yourself, tell your clients.

Did you hit your client's website to gain information about the company? Make that known.

Did you make your client's problem the subject of a thirty-minute brainstorming session with the engineering department? Don't keep that a secret.

Are you getting some extra training, taking a course, or reading a book that will make you capable of better service? Disclose it early in the meeting.

Have you read any relevant books about the client's industry lately? Summarize the key points and share them with your client.

Making a statement like, "I've been reading (blank) and one of the key points for me was (blank)," positions you as someone who is more impressively competent than the last salesperson who darkened his door.

Des Moines–based consultant and sales trainer Jim Lobaito and I talk often. I always ask him what he is reading. "Ask me what I am rereading," he said. If you are rereading something, it has had a big impact on you.

Asking a customer what she is reading can tell you a lot about what is important to her. You will uncover personal interests. It can break the ice and establish some common ground, too.

If you learned math the old-fashioned way, your teachers always made you show your work. They wanted you to get the right answer, sure, but they also wanted to see how you arrived at the answer.

This same principle applies in sales. Clients reward people who have worked to earn their business. Showing your work is a winning strategy. That brings us to this next self-evident truth.

Accidental Salesperson Axiom:
Professionals put a premium on proper preparation.

Corollary:
If you tell them what you did to prepare,
your clients will appreciate you more.

Nowadays, it's common to see television features or even full-length productions that take us "behind the scenes" and tell us how a spectacular movie was made. The director and his company show us their work. They tell us how they created the special effects that triggered awe or perhaps almost scared us out of our seats in the movie theater.

The theory is that value is added when we know what went into impressing us. This behind-the-scenes peek is a new phenomenon. Movie fans in earlier eras didn't want the "spell" broken by being shown the smoke and mirrors. They didn't want their illusions shattered. But people are different today. If anything, modern movie buffs are more impressed when they see the techniques that create the magic.

When the first edition of this book was in proposal form, I remember sitting in an airport lounge where there were carrels with telephones and a place to plug in laptop computers. I returned a couple of calls and mentioned to one person that I had gotten a positive response on *The Accidental Salesperson* book proposal. After I hung up, a woman pushed her chair back from an adjoining carrel and said, "I couldn't help but overhear the title of your book. I'm an accidental salesperson. I was a radiology nurse. Now I sell the equipment I used to use with patients."

I sent her copies of the first three chapters. She e-mailed me to say, "I always prepare extensively for meetings with present or potential customers, but I never really let them know about it beforehand. I have started using your method to start the meeting by mentioning it and have gotten immediate, positive results."

When she read the idea, it made immediate sense to her to market the effort she was making to the client.

Hard work is rewarded, but not if your customers don't know about it.

You have a choice of airline carriers. Your customers have a choice of vendors. It may seem that price is the only point of differentiation in a product or service.

However, in highly competitive businesses, how you sell what you sell may be more important than the product or service you sell.

How does your client know you're a pro? Tell the client what you did to prepare.

The first magic phrase in this book was: "This is the way I work."

The second magic phrase is: "In preparing for this meeting, I . . ." That lets the customer know what you did when he wasn't looking. It helps you become known for what you know and do for the customer.

Why do so many salespeople ignore these two powerful steps in the sales process? There are at least three reasons:

1. Salespeople assume the buyer knows why they are there, so there is no reason to talk about the way they work.

2. Level 1 sales meetings and sales training sessions put the focus on the product and not on the relationship.

3. It has taken so long to get the meeting that salespeople think this is their big chance and go for it all. I've heard this called the "delighted to be invited" attitude. Even if you are delighted to be invited, don't skip these steps.

In this section, you've gained the theoretical underpinnings that solidly ground you in a proven philosophy of selling. But sales philosophy will only take you so far. Now you have to apply what you've learned.

Too many books and too many sales trainers tell you what to do without telling you why to do it. You now know that aligning your sales behavior with what clients *want* will help them see you as a professional. And you understand why it is vital to sell the client on your process before skipping ahead to the product.

Here's a quick way to become known for what you know. Use the template in Figure 3-1 to send or fax articles to your customers. When you mail or fax a clipping on a business issue, first mount it on a sheet that brands your company, and you personally, as the source of this information. You can download a letter-size copy of this form from our website and simply insert your company's logo in the space provided. Use it as a way to provide a "service" touch or as part of a sophisticated system for getting appointments with hard-to-see prospects. I'll detail that system in a later chapter, but start using this tool today.

Marketing yourself as a source of industry information and business intelligence is a Level 3 approach that will help you accelerate your sales success. Having more conscious Level 3 moments is another way to become known for what you know.

Figure 3-1 "Brand" yourself as a source of information in all your communications with your prospects.

TO:	
FROM:	No. of Pages

[INSERT LOGO HERE]

Information about business issues and trends I wanted to be sure you saw.

[rREPEAT LOGO AND ADD POSITIONING STATEMENT HERE]

[INSERT YOUR NAME AND HOW TO REACH YOU HERE]

Yes, You Do Have Time

The "I-don't-have-time-to-read (or exercise or eat right or spend time with my kids or volunteer)" excuse is a lie you tell to yourself and then tell to your spouse or boss. It's a lie because you have time to do whatever you make a priority. So when people tell me, "That's all well and good, Chris, but I don't have time to read," I ask them what they would have to quit doing to have the time.

Tom Hill, teacher, author, and founder and CEO of The Goal Coach Companies, LLC, speaks to entrepreneurs about running a successful business and leading an exemplary life. My wife met him at a TEC (The Executive Council) meeting. Tom tells people who claim they don't have time to read to give a business book one hour: Read the first chapter; read the last chapter; read the first paragraphs and the chapter summaries; look at the illustrations; and if that one hour yields some new information and actionable ideas, you might decide to dig deeper. Just know that you don't have to read every page to extract a book's value. (I might add that it is a quite useful method for evaluating business books; don't try it with a novel, though.)

PART TWO

Transforming Your Sales Department into a Sales Force

CHAPTER 4

Are You a Member of a Sales Department or Sales *FORCE*?

The question I ask any client who's considering sales training is this: "What do you want your salespeople doing more of?" Inevitably, I get answers like:

"I want our people to be more proactive and less reactive."

"I want our people to develop new business."

"I want our people prospecting more."

"I want our salespeople spending less time on personal stuff during the day."

"I want our people to bounce back from rejection faster when they prospect more."

"I want more of our people making quota and fewer of them making excuses for not making quota."

I like personal and organizational productivity expert David Allen's truism: "The better you get, the better you'd better get." It reminds me not to rest on my laurels, and it should remind you that just because you have a "book of business" that is solid doesn't mean you don't have to continually improve.

Back in the late nineties, when I was writing the first edition of *The Accidental Salesperson*, I was doing an upcoming seminar for one of my clients, and I asked the general manager of the company what outcome she wanted.

"Chris, we have some highly paid salespeople who have developed extraordinary faxing skills. I wish they could develop extraordinary selling skills," she said.

With these two sentences she articulated one of the critical differences between a sales department and a sales *FORCE*. In managing by walking around, she had observed that her salespeople spent more time faxing prospects than having face-to-face contact with them, and she was naturally concerned.

She hadn't seen The Chart (see Chapter 2), but she knew that her highest-paid salespeople were reacting to requests and processing business instead of initiating new sales and taking their prospects through the sales process. She had already calculated the bottom-line savings of replacing these reactive salespeople with clerks. The going rate for people with extraordinary secretarial skills was much closer to minimum wage than the six figures she was paying some of her salespeople to process transactional business. She knew that one way to cut the cost of sales was to cut commissions on transactional business (that is business that could be done by fax, phone, e-mail, or e-commerce).

Flash-forward a dozen years, and the VP of a billion-dollar recruiting firm is telling me how, when he visited one of his firm's local offices, he never heard a phone call. "It's just click, click, click," he said. "We don't pick up the phone and call people anymore. We don't take people to lunch anymore. We don't go see people anymore. Click, click, click. We just type all day long."

In *The Empire Strikes Back*, Luke asks the Jedi master, Yoda, "Is the dark side stronger?"

"No. . . no . . . no," Yoda replies. "Quicker, easier, more seductive."

It may be a stretch to call Level 1 the dark side of selling. But you'll have to agree that Level 1 selling is easier and more seductive. Accidental salespeople are often seduced by the "busyness" of their day. When you are selling on purpose, you will put a premium on initiating business instead of merely reacting to inquiries.

Doing Business Virtually May Be
the New Face-to-Face Selling

It is easier to land a sales job than it is to land a major new account. Becoming a force of one in sales requires dedication, training, focus, and resolve. Prospects test your dedication daily and your resolve regularly.

Accidental Salesperson Axiom:

The most important thing you can do is propose your solution
to the prospect face-to-face and ask for the order.

Corollary:

The second most important thing you can do is get
into position to do the most important thing.

That said, the reality today is that a lot of business is no longer done face-to-face. If you've been selling for ten or more years, you may find you are having about half as many face-to-face meetings as you used to. There are three implications of this fact that affect you:

1. Face-to-face meetings are twice as hard to get.

2. You have to master a variety of sales media and methods to connect with buyers today.

3. When you get a face-to-face meeting, you have to be great.

Recently, I was talking to the COO of a small ($9 million) company, who proudly told me, "We sell globally, Chris."

"How many salespeople do you have?" I asked.

"Oh, just two."

"I take it your two salespeople do most of their selling by phone, then."

"Oh no," he said. "Our international guy does most of his selling on Skype, especially in India. He says Indians prefer to do business on Skype."

Face-to-face selling it is, but without the pesky airfare.

When I was wrapping up the first edition of *The Accidental Salesperson* in 1999, I was also engaged in a thirty-five-day, around-the-world seminar tour. I met with a strategic partner in Sydney, conducted a couple of seminars in New Zealand, flew to Berlin for a speech, and ended up for two weeks in England to work with a couple of different clients.

Back then, I did thirteen presentations a month for ten months of the year. Today, I conduct ten to thirteen live presentations *a year.*

I still do sales training, but increasingly it is via webinar and podcast. Businesspeople don't want to have to stop what they are doing to travel to a training session. They increasingly are looking for just-in-time, just-enough training that is part of their workday.

Personal computer software and smartphone apps have changed the way we connect. But they haven't changed the need to approach people at Level 2 or higher.

You can make a Level 1 presentation via webinar or you can "take it to the next level."

Your online demo can be product-focused or customer-focused.

As a salesperson today, you are just as likely to call someone and meet via GoToMeeting or WebEx as you are to hop in the car or jump on a plane to see someone. While the number of face-to-face meetings may go down, sales are more likely to go up. You can reach more customers in more places and engage them more easily using the Internet.

I used to advise salespeople to create a small newsletter and "mail it out." Today, I speak with salespeople who tell me that they connect with prospects on Linked In and Twitter. Salespeople create their own blogs and link customers to them.

There are more ways to connect and communicate today than ever.

Certainly, there are industries where road warriors still prevail and where relationships still matter. And there is nothing like looking a prospect in the eye and getting to know each other over lunch at the club. By all means do that with your top-tier customers. Know, however, that you can serve customers without ever seeing them. You can have business relationships that are both virtual and profitable.

The same principles apply. The way you connect is the only difference.

Call it "selling customers who don't have time to see you." It is a skill you may have to master. Today, the thought of snail mailing a brochure seems laughable. But attaching a PDF brochure to an e-mail is not the answer, either. "Send me some information" is still a convenient rejoinder and a way for prospects to get off the phone with sales reps.

Something you should always ask when someone wants more information is, "Are you online?" Or, "Can you meet me online? I'll point you to a two-minute demo of my product and you can tell me if you would have any interest now or in the future. Fair enough?"

Ask for five minutes. Ask for seven minutes and thirty seconds. Just don't push it.

Becoming a *FORCE* of One

Many companies have sales departments. Fewer have sales *forces*. There are seven critical differences between a sales department and a sales force, as shown in Figure 4-1. To transform yourself from a member of a sales department into a "force" of one, you need to operate on the right-hand side of this chart instead of the left-hand side, which is the "dark side."

It is easy for the accidental salesperson to become trapped by the dark side. Some buyers actually try to keep you in Level 1 and out of their offices by telling you, "Just e-mail it to me," which again has you reacting to requests rather than initiating business.

Prospects protect their time by not meeting with every salesperson. You can understand why. They have come to expect time-wasting, product-focused presentations from the salespeople who come calling. They would rather get that information by e-mail than carve out an hour to meet with an accidental salesperson who wanders in and wings it. By asking for an e-mail, they figure they'll avoid one more time-consuming Level 1 meeting.

Figure 4-1 Behaviors that move a salesperson from the "dark side" into a "force" of one.

Members of a Sales Department	Members of a Sales Force
Have extraordinary faxing skills	Have extraordinary selling skills
Take orders and get buys	Influence decisions and persuade
React to inquiries	Initiate new business
Process business	Take prospects through their process
Have a commodity fixation	Have a high-margin mindset
Meet the buyer's criteria	Negotiate and help set the criteria
Talk to purchasing department	Talk to end users

Recognize and resist this ploy.

A critical aspect of selling on purpose is understanding that the buyer is not all knowing or all powerful. Understand that you have a product or service that solves a problem and that you can bring information and expertise to the table the customer does not have.

You dial the phone and get the prospect on the line. The trap is set as soon as the prospect says, "I'm interested. Send me some literature." At this point, accidental salespeople move into their reactionary mode. They are delighted that the prospect has shown some sign of interest. They dutifully write down the address. They hang up and hurry over to the shelving unit that holds the product literature. They quickly pull ten or twenty pieces of paper from the piles and place them in the company folder. Then it's off to the mail room to have the kit overnighted to the hot prospect.

Two days later, our accidental salesperson is shocked to learn that the hot prospect hasn't read this meticulously prepared package of product literature. In fact, she's not sure where it is.

"It's around here somewhere. Tell you what, call me in a week," the prospect says.

This accidental salesperson is lured into a Level 1 interaction by the prospect, trapped into reacting to a request instead of finding a problem or need. To avoid that situation once and for all, memorize this answer . . .

Magic Phrase

[*Gasp!*] "We're trying to be green and not send out things
Can you go online? I'll get you the information you need quickly."

When a prospect asks for some information about your company, use that magic phrase. The gasp is for fun. You are conveying surprise or shock that someone would ask you to send information.

The trouble with going online, of course, is that you can overwhelm your prospects with more information than they need. So I like to use this time to do some qualifying. So ask:

"What information would be most helpful to you?"

"What concern or problem would cause you to look for a new supplier or solution?"

"My objective is to earn the right to have a longer conversation with you about your situation, so I can be in a position to make an intelligent recommendation. What would have to happen in order for us to meet personally?"

"I have a three-minute video that I would like you to look at, and get your reaction to. And I understand your reaction might be, 'This isn't for us.' Does it make sense to start there?"

There is no one right way to get information to a buyer. The wrong way, though, is to overwhelm your buyers with long demos and Level 1 brochures and price lists about your products and services.

Transforming Your Sales Department into a Sales Force

Transforming sales departments into sales forces is an obsession with me. Let's look at Figure 4-2.

A sales department has many salespeople who have Level 1 relationships with their customers. Salespeople who tend to have Level 2 relationships with their customers will also have conscious Level 3 and Level 4 "moments." Clients recognize and respond to Level 2 and higher behavior. They can tell the difference.

You will be fortunate, indeed, if in your career you have a true Level 4 relationship with a handful of customers. Getting complete trust and gaining access to proprietary information can take many years. However, you can go to Level 2 today with every customer and prospect you meet. You do not want to spend any time (if you're a rookie) or any more time (if you're a veteran) at Level 1.

You never get a second chance to make a good first impression. If you've made a Level 1 impression, your prospects will appreciate the new Level 2 you (refer back to the list of behaviors in Figure 4-1). My firm, Sparque, Inc., markets distance-learning programs for salespeople and sales managers. In one of the assignments, the sales manager coaches a salesperson through the process of preparing and presenting a client-focused, Level 2 proposal to a real prospect. (Chapter 10 includes a proposal-writing template for your use.) Often, this is a first for the salesperson and the prospect. Sales manager Suzanne Reynolds filed this first-person report about how she coached a salesperson through that proposal-writing process. Let's call it "The Tommy Transformation."

> Tommy is a very independent person and not very detail-oriented. He agreed to do the rough outline himself. We planned to go over it in our Wednesday one-on-one meeting. Wednesday came and Tommy had not begun work on the proposal. This was a slight problem since the presentation was on Monday and Tommy was taking Friday off.

Figure 4-2 Transforming from a sales department to a sales force.

	Level 1 Account Executive	Level 2 Salesperson or Problem Solver	Level 3 Professional Salesperson	Level 4 Sales and Marketing Professional
Level of trust	Neutral or distrustful	Some credibility	Credible to highly credible; based on salesperson's history	Complete trust based on established relationships and past performance
Goal/call objective	To open doors; to "see what's going on"	To persuade and make a sale or to advance the project through the process	Customer creation and retention; to "find the fit"; to upgrade the client and gain more information	To continue upgrading and increase share of business
Approach and involvement	Minimal or nonexistent	Well-planned; work to get prospect to buy into the process	True source of industry information and "business" intelligence"	Less formal and more comfortable because of trust and history
Concern or self-esteem issue	Being liked	Being of service; solving a problem	Being a resource	Being an "outsider insider"
Precall preparation	Memorize a canned pitch or "wing it"	Sell call objectives; prescript questions; articulate purpose process-payoff	Research trade magazines; Internet; analyze client's competition	Thorough preparation sometimes with proprietary information unavailable to other reps
Presentation	Product literature, spec sheets, rate sheets	Product solution for problem they uncover during need analysis	Systems solutions	Return on investment proof and profit investment strategies
Point of contact	Buyer or purchasing agent	End users as well as buyer or purchasing agent	Buyers, end users, and an "internal coach" or advocate within client's company	"Networked" through the company; may be doing business in multiple divisions

DEFAULT   Preference settings

I got up, closed the door, and explained to Tommy how the kind of presentation taught in your distance learning course would positively impact his closing ratio and his wallet. We got to work on it together. We went through a rough outline of each section.

He agreed to work on it some more that evening and have lunch with me the next day to show me the final presentation. The proposal he brought to lunch on Thursday was the best I have ever seen out of him. He also seemed to be very proud of what he had done and asked if he could practice presenting it to me in the conference room. He did great! I threw some pretty tough objections at him and he had well-thought-out answers for most of them.

On Monday afternoon, Tommy called from his car to ask for "good luck." About thirty-five minutes later my phone rang again. It was Tommy calling from the prospect's office with a question the prospect had raised that he couldn't answer.

Fifteen minutes later the phone rang again and it was Tommy on his car phone yelling, "We've got the deal!"

The story doesn't end there. Mr. Green, the new client, called me Tuesday morning to ask a question about his order, since Tommy was out of the office. After I answered his question, Mr. Green asked me, "What did you do to Tommy?" When I asked what he meant he said, "Tommy has been trying to get my business for four months now. He has given me a lot of information and specifications about your company and service. One of the reasons I haven't done business with your company until now was because he never seemed very organized, and my rep at the other company was always very organized. I just felt like they would take better care of my money.

"Suddenly Tommy comes in here yesterday and all his ducks were in a row. He showed me that he had paid attention to what I had said I wanted to do with my business, had a program all worked out, and even got the answers to my questions right then, by calling you instead of saying he would get back to me. You know, I saw a whole new side of him," Mr. Green said. "I really like the young man, and I'm happy to finally be doing business with him and your company. Whatever you did to him, do some more of it."

Mr. Green noticed and appreciated Tommy's transformation from Level 1 to Level 2.

You become a "force of one" when you align your behavior with the things your customers value in a salesperson.

Marketing expert Jay Abraham advises us that "leverage" is getting better results from the same effort or expenditure. Tommy wasted four months of meetings by operating at Level 1. Think about that. After four months of Level 1 presentations, Tommy turns it around with one Level 2 presentation. There is a tremendous amount of leverage in moving up just one level. Tommy moved to Level 2 and walked away from that meeting with an order.

That's leverage.

Whether you are going to take the time, effort, and expense of getting in front of a prospect or simply share a desktop, you might as well make the most of it. That means making sure you have a Level 2 foundation for the meeting. It may mean having some Level 3 and 4 moments, too.

A Level 2 approach is 100 percent better than a Level 1 approach, but in the case of Tommy's transformation, a Level 2 approach proved *infinitely* better than his old Level 1 approach.

Mr. Green noticed Tommy's newfound business expertise and image by saying, "Suddenly Tommy comes in here and all his ducks were in a row." He described Tommy's dedication to the customer in these words: "He showed me that he had paid attention to what I had said I wanted to do with my business."

Tommy demonstrated account sensitivity and guidance, in Mr. Green's estimation, because "he had a program all worked out, and even got the answers to my questions right then, by calling [his manager, Suzanne,] instead of saying he would get back to me."

Mr. Green summed it up when he said that he "saw a whole new side" of Tommy.

Your customers can see a whole new side of you today. Your subtle shift in behavior will make a major impact on your prospects. And your income. The fastest way to take your sales to the next level is to identify where you are with each of your prospects and customers. Then shift your behavior by doing one or two things, as listed in the next column to the right in Figure 4-2, to bring added value to your sales relationships.

Star Wars is certainly a pop culture phenomenon. The original trilogy grossed more than $1 billion. Volkswagen advertising now features a miniature Darth Vader who uses "the Force" to start his parents' new car. "May the force be with you" is more familiar to generations of moviegoers than "Here's lookin' at you, kid."

And while you may not always be looking your customers in the face, I have a different wish for you. Here it is. To the company you represent and to the clients you serve, "May you be The *FORCE.*"

You know the way. Just follow your "Chart."

CHAPTER 5

Why You Must Quit Making "Sales Calls"

This is the first book on selling successfully that has ever advised salespeople to quit making sales calls. My advice still stands.

I'll let you in on a little secret. There are "accidental sales managers" who, upon being promoted, become proponents of their salespeople making more sales calls than they ever made. It's something they can measure, and that makes them feel more in control.

For years sales managers have asked their reports, "How many calls did you make today?" Their reports tell them what they want to hear because they end up calling everything they do a "sales call." They delude themselves and their sales managers into believing they are being productive when they are merely being busy. And this busyness rarely leads to more business. As German political writer and satirist Ludwig Börne once said, "Losing an illusion makes you wiser than finding a truth."

When you sell on purpose, you understand that selling is about two things:

1. Making a proposal to a qualified prospect (in person or online)

2. Getting into position to make a proposal to a qualified prospect

Making any move that doesn't help you accomplish one of those two objectives is wasted motion. There was a time when a salesperson could make dozens of "calls" a day. Ride the elevator to the top of an office building and work your way down to the ground floor. Today's heightened security systems in larger cities make this practice, thankfully, a thing of the past.

Flash-forward to today. *Sales 2.0* is the term that describes new trends in selling. Internet technology allows collaborative relationships across a larger platform. Information sharing can still occur in person, but increasingly this sharing is done online and can involve people in multiple locations simultaneously. Proponents say it accelerates the sales cycle and increases sales productivity because a salesperson can interact and follow up with more people more efficiently. I say, it may be the only way some companies will work with you.

Increasingly, it's the way I work today. In the 1970s, I would get into my orange Gremlin and go see my prospects and customers. Today, I can do one webinar and talk with dozens or hundreds of people at a time. That's a great way to leverage an hour. There is no windshield time to take away from selling. I can work, via Skype, with a web consultant in New Zealand. Granted, it's not the same as looking a person in the eye or lunching at the club. But the ability to interact with more people in a day makes embracing Sales 2.0 a smart idea.

When I started selling, I realized that I could leverage each prospect meeting by adopting a higher-level approach (see Chapter 2 on how to use The Chart) that could result in more business without having to make more "calls." Somewhere, there may still be salespeople who close during the first meeting. My experience is that a complex sale requires multiple meetings and involves multiple constituencies. Department heads or buying committee members must "buy in" to the change you are trying to get their company to make. And to buy something new is to change.

Early in my career it occurred to me that I might be better off having multiple interactions with ten prospects at a time rather than having a couple of interactions with dozens or hundreds of prospects. By focusing on fewer prospects, I could maintain the momentum and build trust with a smaller number of prospects, who eventually became customers. I didn't have a way to justify that approach to my sales manager, whose mantra was: "The more doors you open, the more sales you close."

My biggest problem was defining the "new business call" as calling someone I had never talked with before. Years later, when I was consulting for a company, the sales manager told me that he required five new business calls a week. That was in addition to servicing and upselling existing clients. His sales team had to talk with twenty new and different prospects in a month.

"What happens if one of those new prospects wants to meet with a salesperson? And that leads to another meeting or two before you close the deal?" I asked. "Do those meetings count as new business calls?"

The sales manager said, "No, they have already talked to the person, so they are not new business calls."

"But there can be no business until they write you a check," I said, "and it's going to take multiple meetings for that to happen. Are you open to changing your standard? Or, at least, are you open to changing your definition of new business call?"

"I'll consider it," was his reply.

You can see what happens when "calls" alone become what you count instead of all of what I'm going to call "new business moves," which lead to sales.

Adding Quality Rather Than Quantity to Your Meetings

The Chart is my way of adding a quality component to a sales culture that has always focused on quantity. My belief is that you can make more money by having five Level 2 meetings with prospects than ten Level 1 meetings. You can also have a higher closing ratio and a bigger average dollar per order if you have done a good job of qualifying the customer, which requires time and trust. Prospects rarely reveal their true problems to salespeople they don't trust. (For all of the sales managers who might worry about this shift in focus, let me remind you that people won't be working less, they will merely be getting more out of every meeting.)

"Quit making calls." Not the sort of sales advice you expect from a book that purports to tell you how to sell more. But it's sound advice. I vividly recall the day I came to that conclusion.

I had been retained as a sales consultant by a firm that needed one. I asked to see the systems and tools already in place so that I could understand the process the sales managers were using.

"Here are the call [that word again] reports for last week. My salespeople are making a lot of calls, but they're not closing anything," the sales manager said with concern. "Maybe I should have them make more calls."

Although making more calls seems to be a reasonable solution to any sales problem, many misguided sales managers mistake a flurry of activity for real productivity.

After reading several of the reports the sales manager had received, I came to this entry: The sales rep had entered a description of his latest meeting with a prospect. It read, "Stopped by XYZ Company. Ed [the contact] was out. He was having lunch with a vendor at Happy Joe's Pizza. Will call again tomorrow."

I read it again in disbelief. I wondered, why document something that did nothing to advance the sales process?

When I asked the salesperson why he had taken the time to document what clearly was a wasted effort, he said, "We are required to make a minimum of five calls a day and that was one of them." By calling everything he did a call, he was fooling himself and his manager into thinking he was doing his job.

Another salesperson in this same company had entered into her call report, "Dropped off coffee mug as a gift." Chalk up another "call." Only four more to go and she could go home feeling good about how hard she worked. (Or could she?)

See what I mean about the quality of the interaction?

Greek orator and statesman Demosthenes said, "Nothing is easier than self-deceit. For what each man wishes, that he also believes to be true."

And so I began my crusade to get salespeople to call what they do what it is. When all you have to measure is the number of "calls," you get an inaccurate view of what it is you are really doing. Making calls becomes the goal rather than making sales. When you quit counting calls, you can start counting the things that count.

Once I was discussing this very concept with some British sales managers, and they shared with me a story of how a salesperson in their employ had taken to heart my admonition to stop describing everything he did as a sales call. At a Monday morning sales meeting, this salesperson reported to his manager that he had had a prospect "sighting." On Saturday, he had seen the prospect across the soccer pitch, made eye contact, and the two had waved to each other. A "sighting" is the perfect description of what happened. Call what you do exactly what it is.

Counting Your Tasks as Outputs

To sell on purpose you must be brutally honest with yourself about what you are really doing. You do a lot of things to get in position to make a proposal. I like former Intel CEO Andy Grove's idea of looking at the different tasks you perform as "outputs." Not all of your outputs have the same value, although they might all be necessary.

Let's look at some possible outputs and label them. Adapt these "truth in sales labeling" laws and you will never again call anything you do a sales call.

Here are seven sales outputs I recommend you start counting today:

1. *Seeds*. Tally the number of articles on business issues you mail, e-mail, or fax to a customer. For every article you send to a legitimate prospect, you count one "seed."

2. *Letters*. Any introductory letter, thank-you note, or letter to clarify a point counts as one letter.

3. *Dials*. If you dial the phone to try to reach a prospect or customer, you get one dial. Dialing the phone may or may not result in a contact, but you have to start somewhere.

4. *Contacts*. If you accidentally (just kidding) get put through to the person you are dialing or if that person picks up his

own extension, you get one contact. You can get a dial without a contact, but you can't get a contact without a dial unless you are knocking on doors.

5. *Appointments Booked.* If you dial the phone, contact the person you want to talk with, and book an appointment, you get one appointment booked.

6. *Customer Needs Analyses Conducted.* If you have a meeting with a prospect that results in an exchange of information and needs, you get one customer needs analysis. Taking a tour of your prospect's facility counts.

7. *Proposals.* If you present a solution and ask for an order for a specific amount of money, you have made one proposal. The proposal is the most important output you can make. The six other outputs help put you in position to make the proposal.

At the end of the day, you count your outputs. The scenario might go like this: You go to the office in the morning and send out five seeds, write two letters, dial the phone ten times, make three contacts, and book one appointment. Then you leave the office and meet with three prospects. At those meetings you do two customer needs analyses and make one proposal.

You had twenty-four different outputs. You did not make twenty-four sales calls.

Pursuing Is Not the Same as Engaging

To reflect today's new selling environment, I have added an eighth output to the previous list. If this new term gains traction in your career or your corporation, you can dramatically accelerate your sales.

I call this eighth sales output the *scheduled sales conversation* (SSC). It is any scheduled conversation by phone, in person, or online whose purpose is to advance the sale to the next stage in the process. An SSC must be on both the salesperson's and the prospective buyer's calendars. The leading indicator of the health of your sales pipeline is the number of prospects who have you on *their calendars* for an SSC.

You may have a to-do list that's a mile long, and you may be pursuing prospects, but that is not the same thing as *engaging* them. Engaged prospects have you on their calendars for a next step as opposed to information seekers who let you chase them.

Magic Question

"Are you willing to work with me on a calendar basis?"

That magic question lets you know immediately whether you are working with an information seeker or a real prospect. If you have sold for more than a week, you have run into a prospect who says, "I'm interested, but I really have to get to another project (or meeting). Call me next week and we can look into this matter."

You dutifully make a note to call the person next week but never connect. The person doesn't take your call or return your voice mail. You e-mails go unanswered.

That's why the magic question is the best way to qualify for interest. Prospects that put you on their calendars for a next meeting are engaged. People who say, "Call me next week" and won't work with you on a calendar basis are merely in information-seeking mode. That can change, but don't put them in your projections just because they are interested.

Accidental Salesperson Axiom:

Call what you do exactly what it is. Having an accurate view of what you are doing is a powerful success force.

Corollary:

In counting the things that count, you establish ratios to make the right decisions about the activities you need to do more or less of.

Quit Making "Calls" and Start Focusing on "Time Spent Selling"

"Quit making calls" is a startling statement. It is meant to get you to conduct a daily reality check on just how well you are doing. Counting the things that count is critical. Tracking the things that keep your career on track helps you make better decisions on how you are using your time.

In this "age of interruptions," it is increasingly easy to get mired in minutiae. Think about the technology that steals our focus: Conference calls, e-mail, voice mail, smartphones, and web surfing conspire to keep us from completing our high-payoff projects.

"Chronic preoccupation" is a term that I like. It means you are so busy thinking about what you're not doing that you can't focus on what you are doing. Trying to focus on your customer when your cell phone is vibrating is very difficult. Your eyes glaze over and your attention is splintered. Even if your customer doesn't notice, you miss what the customer is saying. That's crucial.

I define multitasking as doing two or more things poorly at once. People who pride themselves on their ability to multitask are rarely as successful as people who bring focus to one thing at a time. Smartphones make us stupid when it comes to relationships. Watch a couple sitting at lunch answering e-mails and you'll see what this addiction to multitasking is doing to our society.

"Got a minute" meetings usually consume at least twenty.

You never seem to be finished. You go home when you are tired, not when your work is completed. It is common in the workplace today for a person to have hundreds of hours of unfinished projects. If you can confront the fact that you can't get it all done, you may at least get the more important things done.

People still buy from salespeople, but prospects are increasingly harder to see. Every move in this book is designed so that the prospect will want to see you.

On NFL broadcasts, you'll often hear a commentator talk about "time of possession." When one team controls the ball for a significantly longer period of time than the other, that team often wins.

There are exceptions, but time of possession is a stat that commentators and coaches take seriously.

How do you increase your sales fast? Increase the amount of time you are having a sales conversation. That conversation can be with a prospect or a customer you are attempting to upsell or upgrade.

You can easily measure your time spent selling (see Figure 5-1). For one solid week, count only the minutes and hours you spend in front of a decision maker. It doesn't matter whether you are conducting a needs analysis or making a proposal. What matters is face-to-face time versus windshield time or computer time.

Have you ever gone home after a long day and been greeted by these words: "Hi, honey. How was your day?" If your answer was that you put out one fire after the other, join the club. You are a salesperson, not a firefighter. You are supposed to be in the field, not in the office.

Time spent selling is an important statistic to keep track of. Because there is direct correlation between seeing your prospects and making sales, your "time spent selling" number tells you exactly how to increase your income: Increase the number.

Putting in time on the job is not what selling is all about. Time spent selling is the essential measurement of how productive you really are. Time spent doing any of the following things doesn't count:

- Flying
- Driving
- Waiting in lobbies
- Writing reports
- Sleeping in hotels
- Checking your e-mail, voice mail, snail mail
- Reading memos from your boss
- Attending sales meetings
- Being trained on new software
- Picking up your laundry
- Taking your dog to the vet

There are so many things that eat up time and distract from the real purpose of selling that it's a wonder we sell anything at all. I challenge you to log the hours you spend in front of a customer for one week. The next week, try to increase that number by fifteen minutes.

Nothing matters more than time spent selling. You are worth more in the field than in the office. And although you should not neglect reading and paperwork, these activities should not cause you to ignore your customers.

One of the fastest ways to increase your sales is to increase your time spent selling. So, learn to time every face-to-face client interaction and log the number of minutes or hours you were with customers or prospects. You can get an even more accurate reading with an inexpensive stopwatch. Use the form I've provided in Figure 5-1, or keep track on the pages of whatever calendar you use.

You now have eight outputs to track and a new power tool—the time spent selling log—to use as an aid. In Chapter 6, I'll introduce you to another tool for tracking your sales process and progress: the Ten Most Wanted List. These reality checks will give you feedback and keep you permanently focused on selling on purpose.

Figure 5-1 Keep a log of the time you spend face-to-face with customers, selling.

Time Spent Selling	Month				
	Mon	Tues	Wed	Thur	Fri	Sat
AM						
PM						
AM						
PM						
AM						
PM						
AM						
PM						
AM						
PM						

Total $ Sales This Month _____   Total Compensation This Month _____

÷ Total Hours in Front of Client _____   ÷ Total Hours in Front of Client _____

= $ Value of Face-to-Face Time _____   = $ "Hourly Wage" _____

PART THREE

Using a Systematic Approach for Every Step in Your Sales Process

CHAPTER **6**

Leveraging the Power
of a Repeatable Process:
Steps 1 and 2

I am sitting in the deli at the Minneapolis-St. Paul International Airport, having a late lunch, when the seminar starts. Without fanfare, the teacher enters the room. He is wearing jeans and a T-shirt. He is not dressed for success by our standards. Instead of a briefcase, there is a bulging fanny pack cinched around his waist.

He systematically approaches people at every table. He's interrupting their lunch in order to make his sales presentation. In about two minutes, he has made ten presentations. His selling cycle requires one more face-to-face interaction to close. He asks each one of his prospects for an order and closes four out of ten. He collects the money (cash!), stuffs it into his pack, and presumably heads for his next group of prospects.

I sit there in awe, analyzing what I have just seen. In two minutes, he has systematically and successfully worked the roomful of frazzled, frequent flyers, closed 40 percent of them, and collected $8 cash! I paid him $2 myself and am now the proud owner of a product I didn't even know I needed.

Having nothing better to do, I do the math on a napkin. Here's the way I worked it out.

$$\$8 \text{ in two minutes} = \$240 \text{ per hour}$$
$$\$240 \text{ per hour} \times 8 \text{ hours} = \$1,920 \text{ per day}$$
$$\$1,920 \text{ per day} \times 5 \text{ days} = \$9,600 \text{ per week}$$
$$\$9,600 \text{ per week} \times 50 \text{ weeks} = \$480,000 \text{ per year}$$

There are more than twenty restaurants at the airport and more than ninety gates. There is a fresh supply of prospects for this salesperson every sixty to ninety minutes, as new flights land or prepare to take off. I estimate he's getting at least a 100 percent markup on his product. By this point, you may be ready to quit your job and join this salesperson. Before you do, let me tell you the rest of the story.

His product is a set of three screwdrivers, each about two inches long, in a plastic pack that doubles as a key chain. His presentation is written on a card slightly larger than a standard business card. It reads:

Hello! I am a deaf person. I'm offering you this handy Tool Key Chain, which may be used for glasses, watches, computers, and more for only $2.00. The proceeds help pay my educational and living expenses. May I interest you in one?
"May God Bless You! Thanks for Your Kindness!"

The illustration on the card is the American Sign Language sign for "I love you."

After putting a set of screwdrivers and his card on my table, the salesperson moved to each table in the room and repeated the process. When he came back to "close" the sale, he looked at his product and then looked at me, raised his eyebrow, turned his palm face up, and communicated this question: "Well, are you going to buy it?" I handed him my $2 and he signed "thank you" and moved on.

I watched as some people shook their heads in the universal sign for "No, I'm not." When they did, he smiled, picked up what could have been their set of screwdrivers, and moved on to the next table and repeated the same process.

Talk about value added. I spent $2 for a set of screwdrivers, and I gained seven free lessons about selling.

1. *Tell people about yourself early.* Establish who you are and why they should buy from you. A little self-disclosure reveals that you are a human being and not just a selling machine. It could be as simple as using the magic phrase, "In preparing for this meeting I did . . ." or else something a bit more elaborate: "I am a deaf person. I am offering you this handy tool key chain."

2. *Recover quickly from rejection and move on.* This salesperson got six *nos* on his way to his 40 percent closing ratio. He just picked up his screwdriver set and moved on to the next table. He didn't take a break to lick his wounds. He didn't go to the bar to drown his sorrows. He didn't stop at the Caribou Coffee stand to have a cappuccino. He didn't convene a meeting of his fellow screwdriver salespeople to tell them how difficult the job is. He went directly to the next prospect and asked that prospect to buy. He kept right on selling.

   I wonder, does this screwdriver salesperson handle rejection well because he has the potential to sell $19,200 a week, or does he have the potential to sell $19,200 a week because he handles rejection well and keeps selling?

   The answer, of course, is "Yes."

3. *Respect your product and your prospects will, too.* While he moved quickly, he carefully placed each screwdriver set on the table. He did that deliberately, with great care.

4. *Use written presentations to help you make a strong case.* This particular salesperson relied on his written presentation. It didn't give every detail, but it made a compelling case for his product. His written presentation laid out the benefits and not just the features. "These screwdrivers may be used for glasses, watches, computers . . ." Sell what the product does and not just what it is. The screwdriver set I bought helped me recently when a seminar participant needed to fix her glasses.

5. *Talking is an overrated selling skill.* This salesperson never said a word and still closed 40 percent of the prospects he approached. Salespeople who can talk often overuse this ability. Listening is a vital selling skill. You can listen with your eyes as well as your ears. The deaf salesperson made solid eye contact and read his clients' body language.

6. *You can sell without smartphones, laptop computers, faxes, the Internet, or complicated closing lines.* You can sell more by seeing more people and asking more of them to do business with you. You need to take who you are and what you sell and boil it down to its essence, and then go make those presentations.

7. *Find a selling system that works and beat it to death.* Put your system on the line so that you don't have to put yourself on the line every day. It may be boring to make that same pitch and sell that same set of screwdrivers to person after person, but could you live on $19,200 a week?

You have a more complex sales process and a more expensive product to sell than the screwdriver salesperson. However, you can still benefit from having a systematic (automatic) way to move purposefully through each step. Beginning in this chapter and through Chapter 11, you will get refinements to help you take control of the dynamics of every client interaction.

Lessons from the Tour

Sarah McCann is my partner and wife. One day she announced that she had booked three seminars in Ireland. What she didn't tell me was that she also had a tour of the Waterford Crystal factory on our itinerary.

"We're traveling through Waterford today. I'd like to go take the factory tour. How about it?" Sarah said.

"Don't we have enough crystal?"

"Are you kidding? We always need more crystal. Besides, we'll never be able to buy Waterford Crystal cheaper than we can at the factory."

Remember those words, because the Waterford Crystal factory tour turned out differently than we expected. In fact, it turned into a lesson-filled accidental sales training story.

ACCIDENTAL SALES TRAINING SEMINAR

The Waterford Crystal Tour

After a forty-two-mile trip on narrow Irish roads lined with hedgerows, we arrive at the Waterford Crystal factory and follow the signs to "The Tour." They are selling tickets for the next tour, which starts at 11:00 a.m. We buy two tickets for two pounds each, and the very pleasant ticket seller invites us to "Please wait in our gallery."

LESSON 1:

Qualify your prospects for interest
and money early in the sales process.

Dazzling is the best way to describe the gallery. You cannot buy anything here. You can only marvel at the beautiful pieces. There's a magnificent chandelier and art-gallery-quality crystal designed by Waterford's masters. There are replicas of professional golf trophies and the crystal football that goes to the number one NCAA Division I football team in the United States.

LESSON 2:

Let your prospects know early on that you have worked with
other prestigious clients. People feel more comfortable when
they know other smart buyers have recognized quality.

At 11:00 a.m., we board one of three buses. More than 250,000 people take this tour each year. About 120 of us are taking it now. As we move toward the first stop, our uniformed guide tells us, in her intriguing Irish accent, that Waterford's aim is not to be the largest crystal maker in the world. Just the best.

We learn that the creation of every piece of Waterford Crystal celebrates a tradition of perfection in craftsmanship dating back to 1783. Little has changed since George and William Penrose first opened their glassmaking factory in 1783.

We enter the "blowing room." Here, huge furnaces transform the mix of silica sand, potash, and litharge into molten crystal. Teams of blowers and apprentices stand around each furnace, where they pour 1,200-degree Celsius molten liquid into molds from which they will blow wine goblets this particular day. We learn that the blowers' skills are essential to Waterford Crystal because of the depth at which the facets will be cut into the crystal at a later stage. Our guide mentions that it takes five years of apprenticeship before a glassblower can make a product that leaves the factory and goes into a customer's home.

LESSON 3:
Tell stories about the founder and the vision.
Don't just sell your product; sell the people who are behind
the product. This humanizes your company and adds value.

The tour proceeds to the cutting room, where cutters work to release the light trapped in the crystal by the intense heat. We see that there is a rough geometric guide of the design marked onto the blank crystal. Very rough. The cutter renders the ultimate position and depth of the cut by his own sight and feel. There are two types of cuts—wedge and flat. We watch the whirring diamond-tipped "cutting" wheels that create deep intricate cuts, the hallmark of Waterford. High-powered vacuums draw crystal dust from the air at hundreds of these cutting stations. The guide explains that it takes an encyclopedic knowledge of Waterford patterns and cuts to do this job. That's because each cutter cuts each design strictly from memory.

There are no shortcuts. No two pieces are ever exactly alike. It takes eight years of apprenticeship to become a cutter and requires great strength to keep the crystal firm against the wheel. There's more. If a cutter goes one "silly millimeter" too far with what is essentially a high-speed, diamond-edged saw, he can put a hole in a goblet or vase. Since there are no "seconds" at Waterford (we learn this in the middle of the tour), the piece is rejected and the cutter loses part of his piecework pay. The goblet is smashed and goes back to the furnace to begin the process again.

LESSON 4:

Build value into the product at every stage of your sales or manufacturing process.

The guide makes sure we see a defective piece. She also shows us the "graduation bowl." To pass from apprentice to cutter, you must put every cut into the bowl. You have three, twenty-hour exams to do it to the exacting Waterford standards. Fail and you cannot become a cutter. Pass and you get to keep your job and the graduation bowl. It's your diploma for eight years of apprenticeship.

LESSON 5:

Market the training your people go through and the standards to which they are held, not just your product.

At the next stop, we observe engravers putting decorations into various pieces of crystal. Waterford has the largest copper-wheel engraving department in the world. Engravers have even more status than cutters and blowers, having taken twelve years to master their part of the process.

I look at my watch as we enter the shipping room. We're about forty-four minutes into the tour. Workers add the distinctive Waterford seahorse logo to the product. Our guide lets us pick up the merchandise to find the seahorse, our assurance that it is made by the artists we saw in the factory that we just toured.

LESSON 6:

Get people involved with your products. Let people in on some "insider information" that not every buyer would know to look for.

In the shipping room, our tour guide explains Waterford's pricing policy. Waterford Crystal doesn't make a piece until it's ordered. So even if we buy crystal in the shop, we can't take it home today. The people we've just seen will make it in the factory we have just toured. They will ship it to us as it comes off the line.

Our guide also tells us that the prices in the shop are the same as they are going to be in Dublin or even Chicago. In fact, the only reason to stop to shop here is that we can see a complete set of every Waterford pattern. Few department stores or jewelry stores can display the whole line.

We board the bus one more time for the quick trip to the gift shop. We go into the gift shop fully aware that there are no "seconds" and no deals. We came to Waterford to buy crystal for less. We buy more crystal at full retail than I could have imagined. And we are not alone.

LESSON 7:

When you take people through every step in your process and build value into your product, price is no longer the key issue. Educated customers buy more confidently and spend more freely.

I witness a buying frenzy as bargain hunters turn into discerning crystal connoisseurs. My fellow tour members queue at cash registers. Salesclerks scan the proffered plastic through the machines so quickly you wonder if it might melt. I marvel at the number of people who thought they were going to get a deal but who are now lining up to pay full retail price.

LESSON 8:

Your own facility is a powerful visual aid. Selling prospects on taking a tour is easier than selling them product. Selling them product is easier after they've taken the tour.

I paid two pounds to take a tour of the Waterford Crystal factory. We paid a lot more than that for the wineglasses, rocks glasses, brandy snifters, cake knife, limited edition vase, and the seahorse souvenirs.

But the sales training was free.

Developing a Sales Process You Can Count On

Buyers who see only price lists and catalogs have trouble differentiating your product from that of your competitors. One of the most frightening words in business today is *commoditization*. When your product becomes a commodity, the customer sets the price and your company loses control of the ability to earn a profit. The strategy of sending your prime prospects and good customers airplane tickets and inviting them to tour your facility is a good one. A well-orchestrated tour can sell more than the same money pumped into color catalogs and ads in trade magazines.

Using your facility and your people as "visual aids" will help your buyers understand why your product is worth what you charge for it, which will help bond buyers to you. An educated customer buys more.

It's more than getting the client on your turf. It's getting the client to see the company behind the product. Seeing where the product is made, who makes it, and how it's made puts value into the product.

Today, you may not be able to get time-starved buyers to your facility for a tour, but you can have a virtual tour online and still build value by educating the buyer.

Accidental Salesperson Axiom:
Selling is teaching. Teaching is selling.

Corollary:
An educated customer buys your value proposition
whereas an uneducated customer buys on price.

By taking us through every step in the manufacturing process, Waterford was able to get full price for its products. When you skip steps in your sales process and jump too quickly to the close, you'll encounter more objections and price resistance.

Have you ever skipped steps in your sales process? Have you ever had someone raise an objection that you could have headed off by going through all the steps? Wouldn't it be nice to have a predictable sales process like Waterford has?

You're about to get just that, because there is a systematic approach that will work for you. There is a system for getting an appointment, a system for planning the first meeting, a system for writing and delivering your proposal, and a system for closing the sale. There is even a systematic approach to after-sales service. It's all here. Some of my readers have shortened the process to seven steps. One VP of sales told me she had expanded her company's process to twenty-three steps.

Creating a "Ten Most Wanted List"

Shortly after the Waterford tour, I began developing a new tool that gives you an easy way to put ten prospects into your sales process and track their progress. If your company sells business to business, you'll need ten business names and, then, the names of the buyer or call point. If you sell business to consumer, you will simply need the names of ten people to call on.

You may get these names from the marketing department or from your sales manager. In some businesses you will be assigned a territory with all of the businesses identified. In other businesses you will use directories, the Internet, and trade publications to find names. One of the best lists of names you can have is a list of customers who have quit doing business with your company. Why? Because you can call them and ask them what happened to make them stop doing business with your firm. And then you can ask, "What would have to happen for you to become a customer again?"

Past customers are great to add to your Ten Most Wanted List because they have already been sold once. Many of them will appreciate your concern.

In addition to putting prospects into your sales process and tracking their progress, your Ten Most Wanted List also puts you in control of making your budget. You quit worrying about one client coming through with a big order.

Here's what I mean. There are two refrains I hear over and over again at most of the seminars I conduct. Someone always tells me that her situation, industry, or customer is "unique" and that none of these principles will work for her. Another person will approach me and want to play "stump the trainer." That's the game that always begins with this statement: "Chris, I have this one client that's driving me crazy . . . ." The player then proceeds to describe an impossible-to-sell prospect who is mentally unbalanced, abusive, or both.

The player asks, "What would you do in my situation?"

Most often my answer is, "If you had ten prospects in process, you wouldn't be worried about this one prospect. You would drop him and go see someone else."

You have two choices:

1. You can worry about that one prospect.

2. You can trust your process.

However, you can only trust your process if you understand the specific steps and calculate the ratios at each stage.

Figure 6-1 is a sample Ten Most Wanted List. You load it with ten prospects and then take them through (in this example) a sixteen-step process.

Please take time to read the sixteen steps on this form. Your selling cycle may be shorter or longer; chances are longer rather than shorter. (Your engineers may have to meet their engineers, etc.) The bottom line is that there is a clearly identifiable process that you take every prospect through.

This one tool puts you in control by showing you where you are with every prospect and what your next step in the process will be. It lets you measure ratios at every stage of your process. In the example in Figure 6-1, the salesperson closed 75 percent of the presentations she made, so you see a 75 percent closing ratio of sales written for presentations made. However, the salesperson started with ten prospects (and presented to four), so 30 percent of the people she put into her process actually bought something.

If you knew you would make three sales for every ten prospects you put into your process, you could quit worrying about that "one account" and begin trusting your process.

You will never know which prospect will buy. Things happen. The prospect you've cultivated takes a position at another company, or his company is purchased by another company whose purchasing offices are not in your territory. You can't predict these things. You can only trust that if you have ten prospects in your process, some of them will make it all the way through and buy something.

Then, take every prospect purposefully through your process.

Figure 6-1 Take every one of your ten prospects through this repeatable process.

Ten Most Wanted List

The 16-Step Selling Process Box Score

Based on your own selling cycle, set a time frame to accomplish all 16 steps.

1. Identify businesses (prospects/clients)
2. Identify decision maker

Column headers (3–16): 3. Seed (describe) · 4. Seed (describe) · 5. Letter · 6. Dial · 7. Contact decision maker · 8. Book first appointment · 9. Confirm the first appointment · 10. Complete 1st appt: Sell your process & frame the issue · 11. Book Customer Needs Analysis · 12. Complete Customer Needs Analysis · 13. Book the proposal · 14. Write the proposal · 15. Make the proposal · 16. Confirm the order (close)

Prospect	3	4	5	6	7	8	9	10	11	12	13	14	15	16
Warner Communications / Sandy Lewin (6/10) / 608-288-3044	6/10 WSJ art.	6/14 USA Today art.	6/18	6/24	6/24									
CBM Companies / Walter Cornwallis (6/10) / 715-223-3900	6/10 WSJ art.	6/10 WSJ art.	6/18	6/24										
Design Concepts / Julian Albrecht (6/12) / 414-221-2623	6/12 G.M. mag art.	6/15 WSJ art.	6/18	6/21 6/24	6/24	6/24 for 6/28	6/24	6/28	6/28 for 7/7	7/7	7/7 for 7/18	7/10	7/18	7/18 $17,354
Royal Oaks / Vicky Mertens (6/14) / 651-748-7085	6/15 G.M. mag art.	6/19 USA Today art.	6/21	6/21 6/24 6/27	6/27	6/27 for 7/5	7/2	7/5	7/5 for 7/13	7/13	7/13 for 7/21	7/18	7/21	7/21 $45,050
Gemini Systems / Fred Atkinson (6/12) / 612-584-9683	6/12 USA Today art.	6/16 left Atlas	6/25	6/28 7/8										
WPSS / Ayssa Jones (6/13) / 412-998-1587	6/13 G.M. mag art.	6/18 WSJ art.	6/21	6/25	6/25	6/25 for 6/27	6/25	6/27						
Network King / Randy Schuelling (6/14) / 608-828-3287	6/15 G.M. mag art.	6/18 USA Today art.	6/22	6/27	6/27	6/27 for 7/6	7/1	7/6	7/6 for 7/12	7/21	7/12 for 7/19	7/13	7/19	7/19 for $5,755
New Frontiers Computer / And Keller (6/15) / 651-388-9522	6/15 G.M. mag art.	6/18 USA Today art.	6/21	6/26 6/27	6/27	6/27 for 7/5	7/2	7/5	7/5 for 7/15	7/15	7/15 for 7/22	7/18	7/22	call in 30 days
Raymond Enterprises / Tom Raymond (6/16) / 715-723-9723	6/16 G.M. mag art.	6/19 left Atlas	6/23	6/28	6/28	6/28 for 7/1	6/28	7/1						
Ermatinger Interstate / Anne Isaacs (6/17) / 612-442-3875	6/17 USA Today art.	6/21 left Atlas	6/25	6/29	6/29	6/29 for 7/3	6/29	7/3						
Totals														

Totals boxes:

Decision makers ID'd ÷ total prospects	Contacts ÷ dials	App'ts confirmed ÷ appts booked	CNA booked ÷ 1st appt completed	Proposals booked ÷ CNAs	Proposals made ÷ prop's written	Sales closed ÷ prospects started
100	**80**	**100**	**57**	**100**	**100**	**30**
% Decision makers ID'd	% Reached	% App'ts conf'd	% CNAs booked	% Proposals booked	% Prop's made	Gross Closing Ratio

Dials ÷ decision makers ID'd	App'ts booked ÷ contacts	1st appt completed ÷ appt's confirmed	CNAs completed ÷ CNAs booked	Prop's written ÷ prop's booked	Sales closed ÷ prop's made
100	**87.5**	**100**	**100**	**100**	**75**
% Decision makers dialed	% App'ts booked	% App'ts completed	% CNAs completed	% Prop's written	% Closed

Beginning the Process: Steps 1 and 2

The various steps you have to complete to close a sale become obvious once you start examining and using this sixteen-step process. In step 1, you identify the company you plan to approach. In step 2, you identify the decision maker. You can get this person's name from a website, the annual report, or the receptionist. You need a name and phone number.

Steps 1 and 2 can be as simple or complex as you need to make them. Many companies grade prospects A, B, and C, according to the size of the business they are pursuing. Other companies may have a figured out what their "sweet spot" is. For example, my sweet spot is medium-size companies with twenty to fifty salespeople and no training department. I also work with larger companies that have multiple locations. They may have a hundred branch banks or sixty-two televisions stations in thirty-one different cities. It becomes prohibitive to train salespeople by flying them to headquarters, so my online delivery system becomes attractive. My experience with companies that have large established training departments is they don't go outside for training. They have too much invested in content development and bricks-and-mortar training facilities. It is an arduous process to sell to them, and usually a fruitless one. So my "A" targets are midsize companies with twenty to fifty sellers and no training department.

If you are a veteran, this is old hat. If you are new, your sales manager can coach you on selecting prospects for your Ten Most Wanted List.

Once you know the name of the person you want to see, you can use the seven-step appointment-getting system (steps 3 through 9 on the Ten Most Wanted List, covered in detail in Chapter 7). When you get an appointment you'll confirm it by fax, e-mail, or postcard. You see the prospect for the first time in step 10. The purpose of the first appointment is to sell the prospect on your process and not on your product. You keep moving through the steps of your process. Every time you complete a step, you note the date.

In the remaining chapters you will learn the specifics of each step of the process. You'll get an effective letter you can adapt for step 5. You'll get a powerful script to use with a receptionist or leave on your prospect's voice mail. These refinements will help you get through to more prospects, book many more firm appointments, make a more powerful first impression, and qualify more quickly.

You can learn a lot about how you sell by examining your Ten Most Wanted List. Like the box score of a baseball game, this tool tells you more than just the score. It reveals how the score actually was made.

When you focus on the process, you also spend less time worrying about closing ratios. Instead, you calculate what I call *advancing ratios*. When you reached a decision maker, what percentage of those calls resulted in an initial consultation? What percentage of consultations turned into presentations? What percentage of presentations resulted in a sale?

Trusting the process is liberating, and tracking your progress is motivating. Too many salespeople have come to think of prospecting, cold-calling, seeding, initial meetings, presentations, and even follow-up as the necessary "evils" of sales. Dispense with them quickly, they think, and concentrate on the important thing—the close. My attitude is just the opposite: Concentrate on the steps and the close will follow naturally.

Tracking New Business Moves Per Week

The Ten Most Wanted List lays out your direct route to sales success. You now know that in order to make one sale, you must simply take one prospect through all sixteen steps of the process. Fill in all sixteen spaces and you have a sale. Chances are you won't move any single prospect sixteen spaces in a week, though. So one vital statistic to track is New Business Moves Per Week.

To count your New Business Moves Per Week, use red or blue ink on your Ten Most Wanted List to note each step you take. At the end of the week, count them. If you move eight prospects four spaces each, you will have thirty-two New Business Moves. Record that number at the bottom of your Ten Most Wanted List.

Then photocopy your Ten Most Wanted List and begin using that photocopy to track your progress. All the dates you've marked to indicate your progress are now black again. On Monday, decide which prospects you're going to advance through your sales process. As you do, use red or blue ink to note each step you take.

In this way, you can see at a glance which prospects you're actively working and which may be stalled.

The point system is easy. You get ten New Business Moves for sending out ten articles, ten more for sending those ten letters. You get ten more for dialing the phone ten times. Still no sales, if that's all you do. But as you keep moving the ten prospects through your sixteen-step process on paper, you advance them through your selling process and get closer to making a sale.

Counting your New Business Moves Per Week gives you a way to focus on the positive progress you've made this week. When you understand the sales process, you gain control and confidence. Understanding exactly what you need to do next with each prospect in your process gives the accidental salesperson a renewed sense of purpose. Every day.

You could move one prospect fifteen spaces and get a sale, or you could move ten prospects two spaces each, or five prospects three spaces each.

You now understand "the game within the game." You can see where you're going and where you need coaching. You may find that your process is bogged down at a certain place—step 10, for example. You complete the first appointment but don't get to the second meeting. That means you need coaching or additional reading on engaging the prospect and advancing the sale to the next step. You don't have a closing problem in this case; you have an opening problem. We can fix that.

By putting down the date you accomplished a step, you build in a sense of urgency for the next move. You also learn how long, on average, it takes to move a prospect through your process.

Once you understand that it takes ten prospects in process to get four presentations and to close 75 percent of those, you begin to trust your process. You don't have to worry about that one account closing. You can sell like you already have made your quota, because you are going to make your quota.

Think about that for just a moment. Have you ever noticed how much easier it is to sell once you've made your quota or goal? There are five reasons this is true:

1. You are under no pressure to close this sale and can therefore relax and go with the flow. You don't have to pressure the prospect or yourself.

2. You project a lot more confidence in what you are doing. When you don't absolutely have to have this sale, you come across as an already successful salesperson. And people like doing business with confident, successful salespeople.

3. You are negotiating from a position of strength. You say, "This is the price" instead of "I'll run your request for that discount past my sales manager."

4. You can be there for the prospect instead of being there for your grocery money.

5. You are having fun and the prospect senses that you are glad to be there. This is a powerful force for success.

The Ten Most Wanted List gives you a formulaic approach to taking prospects through your entire sales process. It's a proven power tool, with precedents in law enforcement. The FBI employs thousands and spends billions of dollars to carry out various investigations. Still, one of the FBI's most famous programs is the "Ten Most Wanted List." Your prospects aren't criminals, but they can be almost as elusive. You may get the feeling that they are ready to bolt out the back door and hide from your phone calls.

If you are serious about selling, you must put many prospects into play.

At the Waterford Crystal factory, we went through every step in the process and paid full retail at the gift shop. Taking your prospects through your process takes the mystery out of higher prices.

Some salespeople resist the idea that they should have a system and keep on applying that system over and over, even though it works. Comedian Ernie Kovacs once said, "There is a classic formula for success in the entertainment industry. Beat it to death if it works." More than 250,000 people tour the Waterford Crystal factory every year, and all 250,000 of them go through the same tour I went through. Beat it to death if it works.

Like the Waterford Crystal tour, the Ten Most Wanted List takes people through every step in your sales process and keeps you from skipping critical steps.

You can download a copy of the exact form shown in Figure 6-1 at my website TheAccidental Salesperson2012.com. Today, having a paper copy of a Ten Most Wanted List seems a bit archaic, so I've also put together an Excel spreadsheet for download that automatically calculates your progress for the week.

You can be working a Ten Most Wanted List or make it a Five Most Wanted List or a Thirty Most Wanted List. Here's the nice thing about a Ten Most Wanted List, though.

It works.

There are many successful companies that have a point system based on activities. At a lunch engagement I had with a branch manager of a multinational imaging company, he told me about the "Daily 75." His salespeople are expected to score seventy-five points a day. You get one point for dialing the phone, five points for having a first meeting, fifteen points for delivering a proposal.

There's nothing wrong with that system, as far as it goes.

What I would add are points for persisting professionally. Two points for getting a referral from a satisfied customer. A point for sending a seed article. A point for sending the second seed. Two points for sending the "Interruptions" letter (which I introduce in Chapter 7). That persistence ensures more prospects get worked thoroughly, and that more one-point phone calls are taken. But that's just me.

I like the idea of a scoring system, though. The purpose is to let you know precisely what kind of activities you need to perform in order to hit your sales goals.

This is a good time to mention another obvious thing most sales managers are oblivious to. There are Level 1, 2, 3, and 4 phone calls and voice mail messages. There are Level 1, 2, 3, and 4 pages of your presentation. There are Level 1, 2, 3, and 4 seeds.

If you send a higher-quality seed and leave a higher-quality voice mail (I'll give you an example of a powerful voice mail script in Chapter 7), you might not have to spend an hour "smiling and dialing" because your number of first meetings will go up with fewer phone calls.

Getting in to See Anybody: Steps 3–9

The screwdriver salesperson can afford to make cold calls. He works the airport and sells an impulse item. I get that.

You can't get on an airplane and start cold-calling. So, generally, the first time you speak with a prospect will be on the telephone. That telephone call won't be the first time you contact the prospect, however.

The screwdriver salesperson has a systematic approach to selling that ensures his success. He has a process he can trust. I am still in awe of the process. Of course, you have *at least* sixteen steps in your selling process, not two. Yours is a more complex sale than the screwdriver salesperson's is. That complicates matters so much that we need to simplify every step in your process.

"Don't Talk to Strangers"

Your early childhood conditioning is the foundation of call reluctance. What was good advice when you were three years old can be a career killer now that you're in sales. You've got to speak to strangers. At the same time, I know calling people out of the blue is daunting. It is much easier to pick up the phone and talk to a person who knows who you are and wants to talk to you than to call a stranger and try to start a conversation.

Not only is it difficult for salespeople to make cold calls, but your problem is compounded because your prospects' parents told *them* not to talk to strangers, either.

In the past, prospects have defended themselves by placing "gatekeepers" in our paths. Today, they hide behind an electronic curtain of voice mail and e-mail. It is easy and impersonal for any buyer to screen out unwanted calls and e-mails from strangers.

Don't worry. By completing steps 3, 4, and 5 (see Figure 7-1), you separate yourself from the pack of other salespeople cold-calling your prospects. You already will have had three (count 'em) Level 3 "moments" before you even dial the phone. Your prospects will know your name and why you are calling when they pick up the phone.

You won't be a stranger. They will want to talk with you.

Obviously, when a prospect calls you and asks for a meeting, you have no need for steps 3 through 9. You already have booked the first appointment (step 10). For the rest of your prospects, you will need the seven-step process that follows.

The Power of Snail Mail—Or How to Get 100 Percent of Your Calls Returned

I am going to suggest something that may strike you as strange in the 2010s. Use the U.S. Postal Service to have a great impact on your prospects and customers. Here's a very simple truth. A short letter with a real signature is real. An e-mail is digital. A busy buyer may deal with hundreds of e-mails a day. The one or two pieces of snail mail she receives will have more impact.

How many personally signed, handwritten notes or letters have you received in the past week or two? See what I mean? Brian Williams reported on *NBC Nightly News* that the average person gets one piece of personal mail—one piece—in a six-week period.

I can e-mail my mother pictures from my vacation. But when I send her a postcard she calls me up nearly in tears to thank me. A three-sentence postcard. But it's real.

Figure 7-1 Completing steps 3, 4, and 5 makes it more likely that the first phone call will be taken or returned.

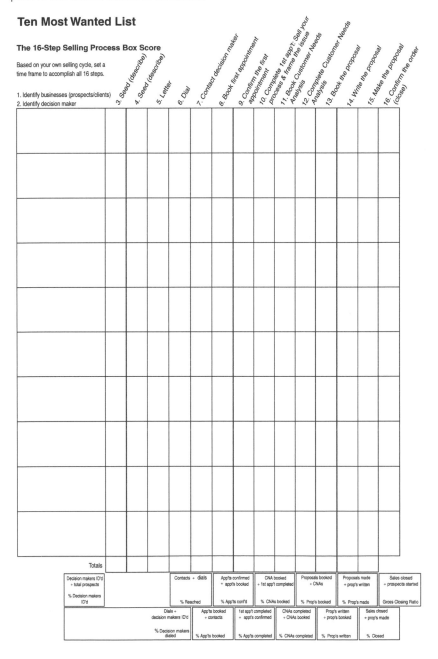

One day I got a handwritten note attached to a *New York Times* article that had been carefully clipped out. The article was about Dick Fosbury's fiftieth birthday. Fosbury invented the Fosbury Flop, which in high jump events is the technique of going over the bar backward. He won the 1968 Olympic Gold Medal with that new, curious style.

The note clipped to the article read: "Chris, as an old high jumper yourself, I thought you would like to see this. All the best, Bud."

The note was from a guy named Bud Stiker, senior vice president, international consulting at the Radio Advertising Bureau, a Dallas-based trade association. In some speech somewhere, I had mentioned that I had been an NCAA College Division all-American in 1971. ("In those days, I held the women's world record," I joked.) He remembered that remark, and when he was reading the paper, cut out the article and sent it along.

I read the article and found Bud's phone number on the note he had written, and called him right away to thank him for thinking of me. During that conversation, he told me that he clips and sends ten articles a week to his contact and customer list. "I send out 500 articles a year. And I connect with 100 percent of the people I send articles to," he said. "They either take or return my call when I call them. Or they call me, like you did."

One hundred percent.

You won't get 100 percent results in getting through to people you don't know by sending them an article, but you will have a much higher ratio of calls taken or returned if you first connect with them in a meaningful and Level 3 way.

Step 3: Your First Level 3 "Moment"

Mail an article about an issue or trend in your prospect's business. Here's the concept: Market yourself and your company as a resource and not just another vendor. Clip an article from a business newspaper or trade magazine and attach your business card to it. Of course, you can also retrieve the article online, but print it out and mail it. Write something like this on your business card: "(Name of contact), Wanted to make sure you saw this," or "Thought of you when I read this," and sign your first name. Then mail the actual clipping with your business card to the prospect. A clipping from the *Wall Street Journal* or an industry trade publication has even more impact than a photocopy. Bud Stiker sent me the article, not a photocopy of the article. This is more personal and powerful than sending photocopies.

Sure, you can attach an article to an e-mail. Or you can fax it over. But I'm telling you what gives you maximum impact is the real article, mailed with a personal note from you.

Send short articles (one paragraph, one column, one page, tops). While your competitors are inundating your prospects with product literature, price lists, and spec sheets, you are quietly establishing yourself as someone who understands and cares about their business and respects their time. (As you may already have realized, sending articles to current customers is a good way to show you're thinking of them, and to keep you in their thoughts.)

By "seeding" the prospect this way, you accomplish three things:

1. You make certain that your first move is a Level 3 moment, by providing information of value.

2. You demonstrate that you are on top of the issues and trends in the prospect's industry. (You did read the article before you sent it, didn't you?)

3. You've put your name (via business card or fax) in front of the prospect for the first time.

Step 4: Repeat Step 3 (Optional)

Two or three days later find another article. Clip it. Attach your business card and mail it. This second "seed" reinforces your prospect's first impressions of you as being different and noticeably better than the other salespeople who are clamoring for her time and attention.

Although advisable, it is not absolutely necessary to complete this step. I suggest you test it. Send five prospects on your Ten Most Wanted List a second seed. Send five just the first seed and go right to step 5. See if adding the additional step gains you a higher percentage of contacts and appointments, and then decide for yourself if this extra step is worth it to you. Whatever you do, don't skip step 5.

Step 5: Send "The Letter"

Let two business days pass and mail "The Letter" (see Figure 7-2). In fact, I strongly suggest that you get this letter into your word processor and into your mail-merge system right now. This is the actual letter that salespeople in my own company use to get prospects to take their calls. Customers have commented that the only reason they agreed to meet with our salespeople was because of The Letter. In fact, a sales manager for a billion-dollar company asked if he could copy it so that his salespeople could use it to get appointments with their prospects.

The Letter is tested and proven. It works.

Step 5A: Schedule the Time to Make
the Phone Call You Just Promised to Make

It goes without saying, but I'm saying it anyway. The Letter works for four reasons:

1. It tells the prospect what you are going to do (dial the phone) and builds more credibility when you keep your promise and call when you said you would.

2. It does not require the prospect to return your call. You are just asking the prospect to alert his assistant that you will be calling. In fairness, then, the prospect must give your letter some consideration.

3. It prepares the prospect for your telephone call.

4. It contains a "magic phrase."

Figure 7-2 The Letter.

3000 Cahill Main • Madison, WI 53711 USA
608.274.0400 •   800.255.9853 •   fax 608.274.1400 • www.lytleorganization.com
Sales offices: Sydney, Australia • Tijuana, Mexico (San Ysidro, California)

[Date]

[Name and Title]
[Company Name]
[Inside address line 3]
[Inside address line 4]

Dear [Name],

Management is a series of interruptions
that are constantly being interrupted by more interruptions.

That's why the reading time on this letter is 27 seconds.

When you meet with me, the presentation is brief and preplanned. It's also client-focused. I want you to remember our meeting as a positive, information-packed experience—not as an interruption.

I will call you on [Day] morning to ask you to meet with me for 25 minutes. This is a non-decision-making, fact-finding meeting.

Good secretaries screen decision makers from interruptions. Voice-mail systems let you pick and choose which callers get some of your limited time.

When you meet with me, I will be presenting information that will help [Company name] [Benefit, e.g., improve its profits]. Thanks in advance for not treating my call like an interruption.

Sincerely,

[Name]
[Title]

Magic Phrase

"This is a non-decision-making, fact-finding meeting."

ACCIDENTAL SALES TRAINING SEMINAR

Free Information

I have replied to an ad that offers free information to people who are interested in exploring a unique business opportunity.

The company, as promised, sends me a free audio file. I am now a lead.

After a reasonable amount of time, a salesperson from the company follows up. She invites me to take the next step in this process, which is to attend a seminar for interested and qualified prospects to learn more about the opportunity.

I resist.

"Chris," she assures me, "this session lays out the opportunity and is the only way for you to really know if there's a fit. And I promise you, this is a non-decision-making, fact-finding visit."

I quit resisting and attend the meeting.

That magic phrase has worked on me for the same reason it will work on your prospects. It positions the first meeting as less threatening and reduces the prospect's need to resist. In your letters and when contacting a prospect on the phone, make clear that you are seeking "a non-decision-making, fact-finding meeting." Discover how many more appointments you land by letting customers feel secure about meeting with you.

Step 6: Dial the Phone

You now have made three powerful and positive impressions (seed, seed, and letter) that ensure you are not a stranger when prospects talk to you for the first time. You have told the prospect, in writing, that you are going to phone on a certain day. Dial the phone. You may reach the client directly. More likely, a secretary or answering system will pick up.

The secretary may say, "Good morning, XYZ Company, this is Heidi."

Now it's your turn to talk. Use this format: "Hello, Heidi. John Keating, please. This is Chris Lytle calling." You will either be put through or you will hear those eight wonderful words: "May I tell him what this is regarding?"

Most accidental salespeople dread those eight words. When you are selling on purpose, you welcome them because you now have a tremendous opportunity to separate yourself from the pack. In fact, that question—"May I tell him what it is regarding?"—is your chance to unlock the vault that gatekeepers guard and get them to put you right through.

You need to say in response: "Sure. He just had a letter from me. I'm following up. John is expecting my call, and I promised I'd call this morning." (Notice how much stronger that statement is than if you were to say, "I represent ACME Widget, and I'd like to set up a meeting to show him our new line.") And you need to say those words with a smile and confidence in your voice. If you expect to be put through, in many cases you will be, because the seeds you planted (i.e., by sending articles) and The Letter that preceded this call have done their work. Other times the prospect will be in a meeting, on another line, or away from the office.

Whether you are put through to the prospect or the prospect's voice mail, in either case, here is what you say:

> Hello, John. This is Chris Lytle. John, you just had a letter from me. I've also sent you a couple of articles. When is a convenient time for us to get together for a twenty-five-minute, non-decision-making, fact-finding meeting? Would a week from tomorrow work for you, say, at 9:20 a.m.?

If you are talking to voice mail, you should repeat your contact information, adding, "Again, this is Chris Lytle at 773-227-3483, extension 202. Thank you." (That's my real phone number, incidentally, in case you have questions about this process or want to share a success story about implementing some of the ideas in this book.)

The key is to ask for the appointment next week. This communicates that you are busy and that you plan ahead. If you ask for an appointment this afternoon or tomorrow morning, you send the opposite message. Prospects want to work with busy, successful salespeople. If you are not booked in advance, you're not busy. Therefore, you're not successful—at least in the prospect's mind.

Another reason to ask for the appointment next week is that the prospect is already swamped. Management is a series of interruptions that are constantly being interrupted by more interruptions. Ask for an appointment today or tomorrow and the prospect can answer truthfully, "I'm swamped. Call me in thirty days."

Asking for the appointment next week, or even two weeks from today, lets the prospect plan that day around your visit instead of trying to squeeze you in right away.

Booking the appointment for next week also gives you an opportunity to skip ahead to step 9. Once the prospect has agreed to meet with you and the appointment is booked, then immediately confirm the appointment (step 9). You don't have to go through steps 7 and 8. You can confirm the appointment by postcard, fax, or e-mail. Figure 7-3 is a sample appointment confirmation postcard.

Figure 7-3 Confirming an appointment makes you hard to forget.

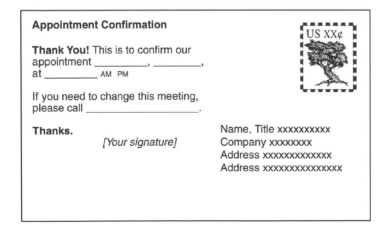

Step 6A: When the Prospect Returns Your Call

Suppose instead that you didn't speak with your prospect but left a message. Know that when you use this system, prospects are more likely to return your call.

When they do, you may have a tendency to say what virtually every salesperson says: "Thank you for returning my call."

Don't say it.

Accidental salespeople say that. When you sell on purpose, you don't do things accidentally. You use words wisely to communicate your point of differentiation on every client interaction. Saying "Thank you for returning my call" implies that very few people return your calls. You are in essence saying, "This is a surprise. It is extremely kind of you, a powerful businessperson, to return a call to a lowly salesperson like me."

That's not what you meant to say. So, instead use this magic phrase:

Magic Phrase

"Hello, _____. I was expecting your call."

The best thing about saying "I was expecting your call" is that it's different. It implies that a lot of important people return your calls because you have something of value to offer.

The first time you say it you may feel a bit awkward. I promise you that after you have said it seven times, and experienced how much better you feel when you do say it, you will never go back to saying, "Thanks for returning my call."

When the prospect calls you back, go at once to the script at step 6 in your system. Here's a refresher, if you need it. With a smile and confidence in your voice, say: "You just had a letter from me and a couple of articles. When is a convenient time for us to get together? Would a week from tomorrow work? Say, at 9:20 a.m.?" Work the resistance. Sell the meeting.

For this prospecting system to work, you have to work it. You will book more appointments on your first contact than ever before. If, for some reason, you don't book an appointment, there is, of course, a backup system.

Somewhere out there, a thousand sales trainers are saying, "Most sales are made after the seventh 'No,' and most salespeople quit after the second one." This system is designed to give you ways to have at least eight interactions before you move on to a better prospect. So if your first phone contact doesn't turn into an appointment wait a week and go to step 7.

Step 7 (Optional): Send Another Article

You want to demonstrate that you haven't given up and that you still believe you have something of value. You can then go to step 8, but you will need to invest a dollar.

Step 8 (Optional): Send "The Lottery Ticket Letter"

The lottery ticket on the letter is what direct mail experts call a "grabber" (see Figure 7-4). The lottery ticket gets the letter moved from the B pile to the A pile. It grabs the prospect's attention and gets him involved with your mailing. It's irresistible. He has to play the game and scratch off the coating to see if he has won something.

Since many prospects open their mail over the wastebasket, the lottery ticket ensures that the letter will be read, saved, and maybe even shown to colleagues. One salesperson booked seven straight appointments with seven lottery ticket letters. She concluded that it works.

Once you have sent this letter, you make the follow-up phone call, following the same script you used to follow up your original letter.

SECRETARY: Hello. XYZ Company, Heidi speaking.

YOU: Hello, Heidi. John Keating, please. This is Chris Lytle calling.

SECRETARY: May I tell him what this is regarding?

Figure 7-4 If the meeting with a prospect is worth a buck to you, send this letter.

3000 Cahill Main • Madison, WI 53711 USA
608.274.0400 • 800.255.9853 • fax 608.274.1400 • www.lytleorganization.com
Sales offices: Sydney, Australia • Tijuana, Mexico (San Ysidro, California)

[Date]

[Name and Title]
[Company Name]
[Inside address line 3]
[Inside address line 4]

Dear [Name],

Take a chance. Meet with me.

I hope this lottery ticket is a big winner. Odds are it won't be, but it's fun to take a chance once in a while.

Some risks are fun to take because they involve a small investment with a potentially big payoff.

When you meet with me, I'll show you a systematic approach to [the problem your product/service solves] that works.

Our business is [Insert your mission statement or slogan if appropriate].

[Name], take a chance. Meet with me for 25 minutes. I promise not to waste a second of your time! I will call you Friday morning to suggest a convenient time.

Sincerely,

[Name]
[Title]

You (smiling): Sure, he just had a letter from me. It had a lottery ticket on it. He's expecting my call, and I promised I'd call this morning.

Secretary: I'll put you through. *(Rings the extension.)*

Prospect: Hello.

You: Hello, John. This is Chris Lytle. You just had a letter from me with a lottery ticket attached. Did you win? *(Listen.)* When is a convenient time for us to get together? Would a week from tomorrow work? Say, 9:20 a.m.?

Sending the lottery ticket letter gives you another legitimate reason to call your prospect. The odds of your prospect winning the lottery with the ticket you sent are very low. However, your odds of getting an appointment go up dramatically.

If you've gone through this appointment-getting process and the prospect still hasn't agreed to meet with you, move on to the next prospect.

Just don't quit too soon.

You may have to send multiple seeds over many months before you get a person to take your call. My fellow trainer Jill Konrath advises a dozen messages over a period of time to build your case.

Just as many prospects resist meeting with salespeople, many salespeople resist using scripts and systems. Choosing your words wisely is part of being a pro. You already use scripts whether you choose to call them that or not. Accidental salespeople say the same things to different prospects. They use the same openings, tell the same stories. Their openings just have less purpose and, therefore, less power.

This seven-step appointment-getting system (steps 3–9) took me twelve years to research, develop, and test. I didn't work on it full-time, but it represents a major commitment of research and experimentation. You get it in one concise chapter. You can get a document with the whole system printed on it by going toTheAccidentalSalesperson2012.com. Just download the "Appointment-Getting Cue Card." Keep it handy and you can approach any prospect with increased confidence because you'll never forget your lines.

It's okay. Pros use scripts. Hey, even David Letterman and Jay Leno use cue cards.

Like Letterman and Leno, you also want to rehearse your lines. You don't want to read your script like a telemarketer selling light-bulbs during the dinner hour. You want to sound natural, and you will, once you have adapted these scripts to your own industry and your own style. If they sound canned, it's only because you haven't practiced and internalized the concepts.

This systematic approach—seeds, letters, phone call, and voice mail scripts—can multiply your appointment-closing ratio two, three, or more times. It requires a little more work than you may be used to doing. But once you set up the system, the system will set you apart and maybe even set you free.

This seven-step appointment-getting system gives you a professional approach. You are not trying to trick people into meeting with you or buying from you. After all, if you were taught the Golden Rule, it will be difficult to do unto others what you wouldn't want them to do unto you.

Step 9: Confirm the Appointment

Let's recap: You've done steps 3 through 6 and, if necessary, steps 7 and 8; you've successfully made contact with the prospect and booked an appointment. Confirming the appointment is one more impression you make before you meet the prospect face-to-face. Your appointment confirmation postcard, fax, or e-mail (Figure 7-3) will go into the "file" (mental or otherwise) the prospect is keeping on you.

* * *

Despite your Level 3 professional approach, the prospect still may resist meeting with you. We'll deal below with some ways to deal with resistance. At the same time, it is possible that the prospect doesn't need or can't afford your solution. Take this prospect off your Ten Most Wanted List and add another. The most important thing to keep in mind is that you are not trying to sell the prospect your product or service right now. The purpose of this contact is to sell the appointment. Avoid getting trapped into making your presentation.

You sell the appointment on the phone and sell your product face-to-face. If there is resistance, you can use these scripts to handle it:

- *Overcoming Budget Worries.* Your prospect might politely decline by saying, "I appreciate your call, but my budget is already allocated."

  Your answer: "I understand. I don't know if we should be doing business or not, John. At the same time, I have some information that can help you right now. I make it a practice to reach out to people I'd like to meet and get to know a little better, and whom I may be able to help now or in the future. I'll ask some questions and listen. In any case, it's a non-decision-making, fact-finding meeting. I wonder if we could get together next Thursday?"

- *Overcoming Indifference.* Your prospect may not outright reject you, but may be incredibly indifferent to your phone call and say, "I'm just not interested right now."

  Your response: "I understand, and at the same time I'm willing to risk a trip and a twenty-five-minute meeting because I have many customers who at first told me that they weren't interested, either. I first had to demonstrate how they could get bottom-line results. Can we get together anyway?"

- *Showing Persistence Without Being Pushy.* If you use one or both of these scripts, the prospect may even say something like, "You're awfully pushy."

  Your response: "John, I sent you two articles, I wrote you a letter, and now I'm asking you to meet with me to see if there is a need for what I sell. I've worked with a lot of companies and helped them improve their profits. I hope you'll agree that I am persisting professionally instead of being pushy. Can we get together?"

If you are talking with a CEO or top management person, you can add this question: "Don't you wish your company's salespeople would approach prospects and persist the way I do?" Said with humor and in the right tone of voice, that question can be a real icebreaker. A typical response is, "I sure do. Do you want a job?"

Generally, top management wants its salespeople to be assertive and go after business just the way you are.

Handle the resistance, and if the prospect says for a third time that he doesn't want to meet with you, be prepared to say, "Thank you. Good-bye."

You do not want to get into an argument the first time you speak with a prospect. You want to leave an impression that you are persistent but polite. It is critical that you don't take the rejection personally. Here's a truism that accidental salespeople have to internalize in order to succeed:

Accidental Salesperson Axiom:
You are not putting yourself on the line when you prospect.

Corollary:
You are putting your prospecting system on the line,
and you can always change your system.

Think back to our screwdriver salesperson, first introduced in Chapter 6. He got six "*nos*" in two minutes. Now that's rejection! He also made four sales in that time.

He didn't put "himself" on the line. He put his product on the table. He put his card on the table. He put his selling system on the line.

This seven-step appointment-getting system works.

Handling rejection is part of the job. *Preventing* rejection means you'll spend less time handling rejection. This system will prevent a lot of rejection.

My Boss Wants Me on the Phone
Instead of Sending Seeds and Letters

I have gotten calls and e-mails from salespeople who have told me their sales manager wanted them working the phones instead of sending out seeds and letters.

"What should I do?" they ask.

"Do what your boss tells you to do, or ask your boss to let you test this system for a month," I advise. You could also spend fifteen to twenty minutes at home doing the seeding and letter writing while doing what your boss says when you're at work. If you are your own boss, I would say test what you are currently doing against my system.

There are Level 1, 2, 3, and 4 phone calls and voice mail messages. There are Level 1, 2, 3, and 4 pages of your presentation. There are Level 1, 2, 3, and 4 seeds. Most sales managers seem oblivious to this fact.

If you send a higher-quality seed and a higher-quality voice mail, you might avoid an hour "smiling and dialing." Your number of first meetings will go up with fewer phone calls. But test it.

The seven-step appointment-getting system covered in this chapter is designed to get you into the office of people who are hard to see. If customers are calling you and you have all the business you can handle, you don't need my system. If someone readily takes your call and grants you a meeting, you don't need my system. And not everyone has the personality, time, or organizational ability to run a system—even one as simple and straightforward as mine. You might want to cut it down to three or four steps.

I am not trying to get you to do more work than you need to do to get an appointment. If you have a powerful voice mail approach that gets your call returned or your next call taken, by all means, stick with what works for you. Let me give you an example of another salesperson's very effective script that you can easily modify to set up appointments to sell your own products and services. Test *this* kind of voice mail script against my seven-step appointment-getting system and decide which one is right for you.

The Best Cold-Call Script I've Ever Heard

You can learn a lot about selling well by being a buyer. I write books, conduct seminars, and maintain a website. But I also own the company. As a business owner, I get called by various salespeople. The most memorable cold call a salesperson ever made to me went to voice mail. It was so powerful I transcribed it, and I'm going to share it with you, word for word.

> Mr. Lytle, I heard a radio commercial about your upcoming seminar in Green Bay. Our firm works with speakers to provide back-of-the-room materials they can sell to increase their daily fee. I'd like to ask you a few questions to see if your audiences—and, therefore, you—would benefit from our materials. Please take my call Monday at 10:00 a.m. when I call to follow up this message.

That five-part message is a clinic on how to create a compelling voice mail script:

1. He told me why he chose to call me. (He heard a radio commercial.)
2. He explained what was in it for me; in this case, increased daily fees. (I'm listening.)
3. He didn't assume that I needed what he was selling; he simply wanted to ask me some qualifying questions.
4. He didn't ask me to call him back. Instead, he took the responsibility for taking the next step.
5. He told me exactly what he was going to do to follow up.

I could hardly wait for him to call me back, because I am always looking for ideas that can help me improve my business. I awaited his call on Monday morning . . . which never came. The lesson: If you have a powerful voice mail script, get yourself an equally powerful time management system to keep you on track.

Time management issues aside, that voice mail is a classic example of marketing the problem for which the salesperson has the solution. Let me tell you one more story about getting in to see anyone. Jim Lobaito runs The Performance Group in Des Moines, Iowa. One of his products is an instrument that evaluates a prospective salesperson for successful sales traits. He has a series of what he refers to as "awakening" letters.

According to Jim, "One day a frustrated customer said, 'I wish the person I interviewed for the sales job would show up when I hire him.'" Jim took that customer frustration and created a postcard showing the person being interviewed from the back. His fingers are crossed behind his back, and over his shoulder you can see the résumé on the desk and the person doing the interviewing. The copy on the front of the postcard asks the question, "Would you like to hire candidates who performed as well in the sales job as they did in the interview?" Then there is a note describing how the instrument he sells helps you uncover real sales talent.

Like my "drip" system of reaching out with an article or two, a letter, a phone call, etc., over time, Jim has a system for sending out a postcard, white paper, voice message, letter, invitation to a seminar, etc., to keep the problem in front of his key prospects. "I have even hired a marketing firm to create awakening campaigns for other products and services we sell," he says. According to Jim Lobaito:

> Awaken marketing [is a technique that] markets the problem the prospect may be experiencing but has not yet acted on. By keeping the problem in front of them, sooner or later it migrates to the top of their priority list. By positioning yourself as someone who understands their frustrations, you differentiate yourself from everyone else who is selling a product or service; in this case, all the other assessment companies. When you get the appointment, you are in position to discuss their frustration and the impact that is having on the customer personally and on the company's sales. It is a much stronger first appointment.

Whether you use my seven-step appointment-getting system, the best cold-call script I ever heard, or a series of "awakening" mailings and voice mails, the goal is to market the problem for which you sell the solution.

CHAPTER 8

First Meeting Strategies: Step 10

The first meeting with a new prospect is your opportunity to gain momentum and move closer to getting someone to write you a check. There is also the possibility that your first meeting will be your last and you will have to fire up the sales process with another prospect on your Ten Most Wanted List.

If you are selling to an individual or selling a low-ticket item, the first meeting may be the only meeting you need to close the deal. Even so, there is a sequence that you follow from greeting the customer to securing the order.

This chapter includes two important tools: a premeeting planner to focus you on your upcoming first meeting and a "Trouble Talk" template, which you can use to create a five-to-seven-minute presentation that will build your credibility so that your customers feel more comfortable revealing their needs and problems.

Establish the Ground Rules of Your First Meeting

The batter hits the ball sharply to center field. It's going to the wall. The visiting center fielder chases it and positions himself for the ball to carom off the brick wall. But the ball hits the wall and—wait a minute—the ball doesn't come out of the ivy. The center fielder throws up his hands to indicate he is not going to go into the ivy to find the ball. The second base umpire rules a ground rule double. There are no arguments from either manager. The "ground rule" at Wrigley Field is clear: If a fair ball becomes lodged out of view in the ivy on the outfield fence, the batter and all runners are awarded two bases (though the fielder must immediately cease efforts to find the ball, or else the ball remains in play), while a ball stuck in the ivy but still in view remains in play.

Before every baseball game, the two managers and the umpires meet at home plate to discuss the ground rules. Those are the rules peculiar to the ballpark you are playing in that day. Since everyone knows at the start of the game what is going to happen if the ball goes into the ivy at Wrigley Field, there are no conflicts to manage when it actually does.

This sports analogy makes a powerful point. When people discuss the ground rules before the game, there are fewer arguments and there's considerably less conflict.

Likewise, when you book an appointment, the prospect is silently wondering:

- What's going to happen?
- What are your credentials?
- How long is this meeting going to take?
- When is the close coming?

The best advice I can give you is to answer those questions early in the first face-to-face meeting you have with the prospect. And consider doing it even after the prospect becomes a customer. By discussing your agenda and describing your process (the way you work) up front, you make a small but very important first sale. You sell the prospect on the way you are going to work together. You establish the ground rules.

The First Meeting Is the Time to Sell Your Process and Frame the Issues

You gain credibility by revealing your sales process. The fact that you have a process sets you apart from many accidental salespeople. By being clear about the way you work, you let the customer buy into the process before buying your product.

Skipping this one step stalls many salespeople in their tracks. Accidental salespeople feel they are lucky to have an appointment. They skip the vital step of setting the ground rules and selling the prospect on the way they work. When you sell on purpose, you explain your process before you explain your product.

Stand Out from the Parade of Salespeople Calling on Your Customer

For three years, I was the marketing director of a major Wisconsin-based retailer. Part of my job was buying advertising for the company. For the first six months, I kept count in a log and discovered that 168 salespeople had called on me in that period. Thirty years later I vividly recall that only two of them (Tom Fiewigger and Mark Strachota) approached me professionally. Each came to the meeting with an agenda. They went over the points they wanted to accomplish and told me how long it would take. They always got more of my attention and a larger percentage of my budget than the parade of accidental salespeople who passed through my office.

Some of the accidental salespeople took a deep breath, sat back in the chair across the desk from me, and settled in like my office was some kind of rest stop. They seemed to be there to gather strength for their next meeting. They certainly weren't prepared for the present one: "So, Chris, what's going on?" they would ask "Anything coming down for me this week?"

Mack Hanan writes many sales books, and one of his book titles says it all: *If You Don't Have a Plan, Stay in the Car.* Even if you never cracked open Mack's book, you would know never to approach a prospect without a premeeting plan.

If you don't have a plan, stay in the car—and work on your plan. When you get that face-to-face meeting with the prospect, reveal your plan. The first face-to-face encounter is the best time to use the first magic phrase: "This is the way I work."

Share with the prospect what you want to accomplish. Tell her how much time you want. Describe the steps you will take to make an intelligent proposal.

Quit hiding your agenda. Get it out in the open early.

Tell the truth.

And whatever you do, don't apologize for being there or say, "Thank you for your time." Your time is just as valuable as the prospect's. Avoid trite phrases like, "I'm not here to sell you anything." Because that is exactly what you are there for.

Accidental salespeople say those things because they don't know any better. You do. You now use these magic phrases to set yourself apart.

"In preparing for the meeting I . . ."

"This is the way I work."

"This is a non-decision-making, fact-finding meeting."

Believe me, buyers can feel the difference when they are approached with purpose. Salespeople who walk in the door unprepared and without interest or purpose show very little curiosity about the prospect's business. Their purpose (such as it is) for being there is to see what is happening, not to make something happen. "Your account has just been assigned to me," said one salesperson as he walked into my office. (*All right*, I thought to myself, *another new salesperson to break in.*) The approach that evidences a complete lack of interest or purpose is when the salesperson says, "I was just in the area and I thought I'd drop by to see if you need anything." You've been warned. By purposefully avoiding the two things buyers dislike the most, you instantly separate yourself from the pack of accidental salespeople who just don't get it.

This next tool will help you have a very productive first meeting.

Use a Premeeting Planner

I have always been a "toolmaker." I realized a long time ago that speaking or writing about sales is not enough. By including tools that help you put the learning into action, I can get you to do something instead of just know it. Education without action is entertainment. To know and not to do is not to know.

The premeeting planner in Figure 8-1 gives you an immediately actionable sales tool. Neil Rackham, author of *SPIN Selling*, differentiates between simple and complex sales. Most of you make complex sales that require multiple meetings and involve long-term commitments for big-ticket products and services. Chances are you will meet with more than one decision maker during the selling process.

Because you have to "advance" the prospect through your sales process, you have to ask for a lot of things before you ask for the order. Pay close attention to the third question in Figure 8-1: "Have I given, or can I give, the customer a premeeting assignment?" Accidental salespeople tend to be shy about asking for too much or probing too deeply. When you start selling on purpose, you will ask your prospect to do little things for you. You want to start with easy things for them to say "yes" to, and progress to higher-risk, higher-payoff "asks." Within reason, prospects will do low-risk things for you if there is some benefit in it for them.

It makes sense. A prepared prospect is a better prospect. But unless you ask prospects to prepare, odds are they won't.

What do we know for sure? Your prospects are busy people. They don't sit around thinking about what you are doing or how the next meeting with you is going to go—unless you ask them to. There is nothing worse than showing up for that first meeting all prepared and excited and have the customer greet you by looking at his Outlook calendar and then looking up and saying, "Oh, it's you."

That's your tip-off that he hasn't thought about the meeting since you booked it. And if the customer didn't think about this first meeting from the time you booked it to the time you walk into the office, you will have to do a lot more heavy lifting to get him engaged.

An e-mail, fax, or written note that gets the prospect to complete a small task before your first meeting (or any meeting, for that matter) puts you at a subtle advantage. Instead of just confirming your upcoming meeting (always a good idea), consider giving the prospect a specific task to prepare to make the meeting more productive. Here are two examples of how a fax or an e-mail might read:

Figure 8-1 Ladies and gentlemen, I have completed all of my premeeting checks.

Premeeting Planner

Client

Date

One major difference between top performers and moderate performers in any field—and especially in sales—is the way they prepare to do their jobs.

Precall planning is not just thinking about what you will say. It is creating the qualifying questions you will ask and deciding what information you will share.

You're not selling your product or service; you're selling a solution to your prospect's problem. So first you've got to discover a problem you can solve, and to do that you'll need to ask some strategic questions.

Precall planning lets you determine what success means before every call instead of after the call.

How can I manage this sale?

1. At what stage of the process am I with this prospect? (Steps 1 through 16)

2. What new business moves can I make with this prospect today?

3. Have I given or can I give the prospect a premeeting assignment?

4. Have I completed all the steps to this point? Anything need to be firmed up?

5. What can I read, research, or do to have a Level 3 "moment" with this prospect? (Trade press, Web site, etc.)

6. If this meeting is successful, what will happen?

7. What will I ask the prospect to do?

8. What is my fall-back position if the customer says "No" to my first ask?

9. What evidence will I bring to the meeting to support my position?

10. What are the benefits to the prospect for doing what I'm suggesting?

11. What questions will I ask?

12. What information will I share?

13. What preparation will I tell the client about?

14. Should I open the meeting with the words, "In preparing for this meeting, I . . ." ?

15. How can I frame the issues?

16. What do I want to know about the prospect's company?

17. What do I want to learn about the prospect?

18. What information do I want the prospect to know about me? (Self-disclosure)

19. Do I have Level 3 and 4 information to present as well as Level 1 and 2?

John,

Looking forward to our meeting tomorrow at 9:00 a.m. I plan to explore these issues. How do you rate the level of service you are getting from your current supplier? What does "good" look like? What does "excellent" look like, from your perspective? In order to save time tomorrow, please take a few minutes to think about that today. Thanks.

Chris

Mary

See you at 11:00 a.m. on Tuesday. In preparing for our meeting, I came across an article that I'd like to discuss. Would you please skim this article and give me your reaction to the highlighted segment when we get together?

Chris

Giving the prospect a premeeting assignment can be as simple as sending over the four or five bullet points of your agenda by e-mail and asking the customer to add his agenda items to it. Even if the prospect doesn't add agenda items, he's read your ideas and thought about the meeting. That's the point.

There are at least six premeeting assignments I can recommend:

1. Ask the prospect to reserve a conference room with an LCD projector or to have her assistant let you know if you need to bring your own equipment.

2. Ask the prospect to invite other decision makers or stakeholders to the meeting.

3. Ask the person you are meeting with to read a short article before the meeting, especially if the article gives evidence of a problem that is common in the prospect's industry.

4. Ask the prospect to visit your website to look at a specific piece of information. Send the link.

5. Ask the prospect to call one of your satisfied customers before the meeting. Or ask a satisfied customer to call your prospect on your behalf.

6. Ask the prospect to think about the answer to a specific question you pose in an e-mail.

Control the things you can control before and during an appointment. You can control how much you prepare. You can plan the meeting and set goals for it. You can ask the prospect to prepare to get the most out of the meeting. You can share your agenda with the prospect. All of these little things make a big difference. Admittedly, reading an article is a small, low-risk task to ask of the prospect. Get your prospects used to doing little things you ask. By the time you ask for the order, they will be used to doing what you ask them to do.

Just like a pilot using a preflight checklist, you can think through any upcoming meeting using a premeeting planner. Use it to note your goals and to play the meeting in your head before it happens. See yourself sharing your agenda and information. If you have a very important meeting coming up, then I suggest you work through each point on your planner instead of just thinking it through. Write down your important points and practice talking about them in advance. When you have to explain something out loud to another individual, you have to be very clear, especially when you have an upcoming scheduled sales conversation. However, if this is your first meeting with a prospect, you may want to "frame the issues" before you move to the customer needs analysis, which is a distinctly new step (which we'll cover in the next chapter), but may flow naturally from and occur in the first meeting.

Here's why you want to establish your credibility first: People have a hard enough time talking to strangers. Think about how hard it is for them to reveal their problems to a stranger.

One of my favorite cartoons shows a couple sitting in front of a desk. Seated at the desk is the marriage counselor. The caption reads: "Well, Doc, besides money, in-laws, and sex, we don't really have any serious marital problems."

Therapy is an interesting process. You pay a counselor a hefty fee to listen to your problems and you still may hide the problem from the therapist for months, or even years, until you feel comfortable enough to confront the real issue.

Of course, you're not a therapist, and a majority of your prospects probably don't need therapy. Still, buyers don't reveal their real needs and problems to salespeople they have just met and have no reason to trust. Period.

The consultative process has become ingrained in the collective sales consciousness. We have trained salespeople to ask questions first to discover a problem or need. Then, and only then, should you talk about your product, process, or service. The question remains: *Why* should prospects answer your questions and reveal their problems to you? This is the first time they have ever laid eyes on you.

Do You Have a "Trouble Talk" Presentation?

The way to establish credibility is to have a credibility presentation. Its purpose is to break the customer's preoccupation with whatever is top-of-mind and get her to think about a problem you can solve.

That's what traveling salesman Professor Harold Hill did in the stage musical (and, later, the film and television production) *The Music Man*, when he got to River City, Iowa.

Even if you have never seen *The Music Man*, you must have heard the song "Trouble." "Trouble that starts with a capital T and that rhymes with P and that stands for Pool." (You can go to YouTube and search for "Music Man Trouble" and get up to speed very quickly—four minutes, eleven seconds to be exact.)

River City was doing just fine without a boys' band, but Professor Hill quickly got the citizens of River City concerned enough to consider one. In the song "Trouble," Harold Hill gives us a powerful demonstration of how to frame the issues. He's looking for a problem, an angle. He needs an opening so that he can launch his sales pitch.

"You remember the pitch," Hill says. "What's new around here? If I'm going to get your town out of the serious trouble it's in, I'll need to create a desperate need in your town for a Boys' Band."

It turns out there's a new pool table over at the Pleez-All Billiard Parlor, and that's the only opening Hill needs. "Either you are closing your eyes to a situation you do not wish to acknowledge," he says. "Or you are not aware of the caliber of disaster indicated by the presence of a pool table in your community. Well, you've got trouble, my friend...."

After getting the townsfolk worried about the deleterious effect a pool table might have, Hill paints a picture of a parade led by town kids playing "76 Trombones." He builds alliances, gets the city council on his side, and ultimately sells his band instruments by the Wells Fargo wagonload to the townsfolk.

The Music Man details the power of framing the issues for an entire town. Instead of starting with his product, Hill starts with the implications of having a pool table in River City. That's lesson one: *Frame the issue.* You can gain credibility and rapt attention by framing the issues for your prospect before you do a customer needs analysis or make a written proposal or presentation.

There are two other lessons I missed the first ten times I watched *The Music Man*, which turns out to be a pretty good sales training film. Lesson two is: *Don't be afraid of a tough territory.* The other salespeople Professor Hill meets on a train into town opted to stay on the train and bypass River City rather than trying to sell to Iowans. As a result, he had no competition. Harold Hill saw Iowa as a personal challenge to his sales skills.

The third and final lesson is: *Sell concepts instead of products.* While Professor Hill did not always use the most ethical sales tactics, if you simply dismiss him as a con man you miss one of the most valuable lessons from the film: Hill was selling a concept. He understood that he was not selling trombones and trumpets. He had a much more important concept: He sold "a way to keep our children moral after school." Once the River City citizens bought that concept, they couldn't part with their money fast enough.

Peter Drucker, known as "the man who invented management," told us that "the customer rarely buys what the business thinks it's selling. Top performers in every industry sell concepts. That is why they are top performers."

Professor Harold Hill was a pitchman. Today's sales techniques have evolved from pitching to consulting. At the same time, we've left behind some of the good things the pitchman brought to the table—things like passion and painting vivid pictures of a better way of life. Professor Hill is a spellbinder. He's his own visual aid. He creates a vision of a River City Boys' Band and gets the towns-folk to imagine a better way of life.

Pitching product is different from finding real needs and filling them. On the other hand, being able to find a problem and create urgency has become almost a lost art. Accidental salespeople go into a prospect's office to see what's happening. Harold Hill went into River City to *make* something happen. Watch the film from that perspective and you'll absorb valuable sales lessons.

Successful salespeople use stories, metaphors, and analogies in-stead of catalogs, spec sheets, and price lists. They paint vivid pic-tures of a better way of living or doing business. They get people to imagine the enjoyment of a better life before they actually have it.

During the first appointment, you want prospects to feel at ease with you. You also want them to become somewhat ill at ease with the status quo. You want to frame some issues and point out the "trouble" they may be in if they don't take action. In order to frame the issues for a prospect, you need an all-purpose "Trouble Talk" or credibility presentation that should focus on real problems that peo-ple face if they don't implement your solution.

As a speaker and trainer on sales, when I meet with a prospect for the first time, I'll often send a copy of The Chart (see again Fig-ure 2-1) ahead of time, and I always carry a copy with me. Then my Trouble Talk goes something like this:

> My experience is that most people get into sales accidentally. They don't want to be seen as pushy salespeople. After all, the only salespeople portrayed in the media are high-pressure types with low self-esteem. That's not how they want to be seen, so they default to Level 1 on The Chart. They don't understand that the opposite of pushy is professionally persistent. Does that make sense?

Our programs and processes help teach your accidental sales-people how to sell on purpose. We set their preference at Level 2 and show them how to have conscious Level 3 and 4 "moments." That helps them leverage their results at every stage of your selling process.

When I move into the consultation phase, I'll ask the prospect how many members of his team are operating at Level 1. Now he's using my model to answer questions about his problems.

"Can you see that some of your salespeople are operating at Level 1?" I'll ask

"Chris, I have four Level 1 people on my team, and one of them is our top producer."

By framing the issues and using my model to discuss the prospect's problem, I have established more trust and credibility. (Sometimes I'm tempted to say, "Well, you've got trouble, my friend.") Sharing information is not the same as presenting your solution.

Do you have a Trouble Talk presentation ready? Can you frame the issues for a buyer? There is a lot to be said for listening to the prospect. Still, there also is something to be said for having *something to say* to the prospect to build credibility and trust. When prospects see you as a person who knows what you are doing, they will reveal more to you.

Complete the sentences in the template provided, and you are on your way to having a Trouble Talk of your own. After you deliver your Trouble Talk, you will have a prospect who is more willing to go through your process.

TROUBLE TALK TEMPLATE

One of the problems that costs businesses a lot of (money, time, hassles) is _____.

Left unchecked it can _____.

According to research by _____, this problem is . . . .

One of our customers documented a savings of _____ by (*tell a story.*)

My observations/experiences have been _____.

Moreover, research indicates that _____.

It is especially costly in terms of lost _____.

Unchecked, it leads to _____.

But it doesn't have to be that way. Hundreds (thousands) of customers are benefiting from _____ because . . .

Our research into the problem has caused us to approach the problem by _____.

Would you be willing to explore how _____ could help you improve your _____?

Your Trouble Talk should allow you to share stories and paint pictures of happy customers enjoying the benefits of using your product or service. You can help them visualize the problems they will continue to deal with if they don't use your offering. When the prospect sees he is not alone in his distress, and that you have helped others in his situation, you are more likely to have a more productive, fact-finding session or needs analysis (step 11).

The Trouble Talk gets the customer to focus on a problem or business issue that he faces. That's a better starting point for the first meeting than doing a demonstration of your wonderful product or service. It frames the issues and establishes your credibility. You want the customer laser-focused on the problem. Once you have established that there is a problem, you are much more likely to be the one to sell the solution.

I have learned a lot about selling by being sold by great sales pros. Admittedly, buying a pair of pants doesn't require a sixteen-step sales process. But I include this example here to show the power of getting the customer (me, in this case) to quit focusing on price and start focusing on the problem.

ACCIDENTAL SALES TRAINING SEMINAR

The Black Pants

My wife, Sarah, is picking me up at O'Hare and we are spending our anniversary weekend in Chicago. The plan is to have dinner out at two new restaurants and enjoy a nonwork weekend together in a nice hotel.

"I don't want you to wear one of the blue suits that you always speak in, so I packed the new linen jacket I got you for Christmas and some slacks," my wife tells me. As I unpack I discover that the slacks are the ones I've outgrown. They fit when I bought them, but today they are a little snug in the waist.

I could get them on, but I couldn't sit down. So it is a problem. "Of all the black slacks that are hanging in my closet, why did you pack these?" I ask.

"Because they were in your closet. Why were they in the closet if they don't fit?"

"I'll lose the weight some day. Tell you what, I'll just wear this suit to dinner."

"Oh no, you won't," she says. "I visualized this dinner and you're wearing the jacket. We're going to go shopping and get you a new pair of black pants."

Our hotel is on Michigan Avenue and outside the door is one store after another. The first four stores do not have a pair of black slacks in my size. It is now about 6:45 p.m. We walk into Lord & Taylor in Water Tower Place.

The salesperson approaches and I pretty much tell him the story you've been reading. I say, "I need a pair of black pants, 38 waist, 34 inseam. They should cost no more than $40."

The salesperson doesn't flinch. He goes off and looks through the racks of slacks. When he comes back he says, "Sir, I couldn't find anything in your size in that price range." (Note that he could just as easily have said, "We don't have anything that cheap in the store.") But he adds, "May I show you what I found?"

"You may show me, but I want a $40 pair of pants."

With great flourish, he drapes the legs of the pants over one arm and presents them almost as though they were a bottle of fine wine (which I'm anticipating having at the restaurant I am trying to get to).

"Do you know the Burberry brand, sir?"

"Listen, I've got *suits* that cost less than that pair of Burberry pants. I just want a nice pair of $40 precut pants today."

"Sir, do you ever wear braces?" he says, ignoring my whining.

"Occasionally."

"Good, because these have the braces buttons already sewn in. They have an interior lining to the knee so that they will hold the crease longer and require less dry cleaning and pressing. That will save you money in the long run."

"Okay, how much?"

"Sir, they are only $120."

"Look, I appreciate the quality, but I have several pairs of black pants hanging in my closet at home. I just want some $40 pants."

"I understand. Shall we make this your backup pair?"

Now I'd never heard of a "backup pair" of pants. "What do you mean?"

"Well, it means that you can shop for a while longer, and if you can't find another pair of pants, these will be here for you."

"This is my backup pair, then," I agree.

As I turn to walk to yet another store, he asks another question.

"By the way, what time is your function?"

"Our reservation is for eight o'clock." I realize I have only seventy-five minutes until dinner.

"The reason I ask is that these pants have to be tailored. Where are you staying?"

"Just down the street at the Hyatt."

"Good. If I can get the tailor to work on them, you could get back here fairly quickly."

(Now I'm mentally down another twenty minutes.)

"How far is it from your hotel to the restaurant?" he asks. Sarah points out that it's a good fifteen minutes.

"Before you go, just let me make sure I can get them tailored fast enough if you do decide to buy." He picks up a phone and starts an animated discussion with someone on the other end. To this day, I believe it is the tailor.

"No, tonight.... Uh-hum.... It's his anniversary. Can you do it?"

Now he's selling the tailor on going to work for me, putting my project at the top of a huge list of alterations.

"I'll ask," he says into the telephone. Then, turning to me, asks: "Straight legs or cuffs, sir?"

"Straight legs are fine," I say, knowing that I have just invested in a pair of Burberry pants.

"I'll run them right down to the tailor. Will that be Lord & Taylor charge or some other method of payment?"

He sold me a pair of pants for $120. The sales seminar he put on was free, a value-added clinic on keeping the customer focused on the problem. He kept framing the issues for me. All of a sudden, he was selling the concept of my getting to my function on time and looking good, instead of justifying the price.

My anniversary dinner was saved, and although I've thrown out a lot of other mementos, the black pants still hang in my closet.

Accidental Salesperson Axiom:
When you control the focus of the meeting,
you control the meeting.

Corollary:
Keeping the focus on the prospect's
problem helps you sell faster.

The salesperson framed the issues for me. I could keep looking for a pair of $40 pants or I could take action. He let me know what would happen if I kept looking. He kept me focused on my date, my dinner reservation, my travel time.

He also did a brilliant job of asking questions and keeping the sale open long enough to get it closed, which we will deal with when we talk about qualifying the prospect in the next chapter.

Trouble Talk gives you a place to start when the customer doesn't come to you with a problem. It lets you shift the customer's attention from his preoccupation with the problem he was dealing with when you walked in to the problem you can solve for him.

One more thing: Trouble Talk should add value to the customer's day even if he doesn't buy from you.

There are full-size copies of each of these two power tools, the premeeting planner and the Trouble Talk template, at www.TheAccidentalSalesperson2012.com.

CHAPTER 9

Transitioning from Needs Analysis to Proposal Meeting: Steps 11–13

You have identified the business you wanted to sell to and found the name of the decision maker (steps 1 and 2). You have worked as many steps of the seven-step appointment-getting system (steps 3–9) as you needed in order to secure the first meeting, at which you deliver your short Trouble Talk presentation to gain credibility (step 10). So, where do you go from here?

Assuming the meeting is going well, you don't go anywhere. You transition into the customer needs analysis (step 12), which means you skip step 11.

Step 11 on the Ten Most Wanted List is to book the needs analysis meeting. Let's say you are twenty minutes into the first meeting. You have delivered your Trouble Talk and the prospect has expressed some interest in addressing a particular problem or need.

"It sounds like you would like to address this issue," you say. "May I ask you a few more questions about it, so I can be in a position to make some intelligent recommendations?"

If the prospect's answer is yes, you have automatically moved to step 12, which is the customer needs analysis meeting itself. If the prospect's answer is no, you need to book your second meeting to get to step 12.

Step 11 and step 13, booking the needs analysis and proposal meetings, only take a few seconds each. Why bother putting them into the sixteen-step system? Because if you leave a meeting without having the next meeting on both calendars, you are going to lose momentum. In golf, you count one stroke whether you hit a 300-yard drive or tap in a three-inch putt. To me, steps 11 and 13, while very short ones, are important enough to merit their own distinct step in the process.

Going Where Your First Meeting Takes You

Many of us have been in meetings that we thought were going pretty well when the person across the desk looks at his watch and says, "I've got to jump on another conference call. But this looks good. Give me a call early next week and we can continue our discussion." (If you've never had this happen to you, just skip the next paragraph.)

Remember to ask the magic question to those prospects who suggest they are interested:

"Are you willing to work with me on a calendar basis?"

I want to reiterate there is a clear distinction between prospects and information seekers. Prospects put you on their calendar for a next step. They are engaging with you. Information seekers let you chase them down, they avoid your phone calls, and they occasionally engage by e-mail. If I were your sales manager, I would not put an opportunity of yours into my projections unless you had a "scheduled sales conversation" on your calendar. People who don't engage with salespeople rarely buy, even if they say they are interested.

If you cannot close the sale during a meeting (whether it is the first meeting or any subsequent meeting you have with the prospect), then close on the date and time of the next meeting. That is your fallback position. If you cannot close on that next scheduled sales conversation, you may have to terminate the process with that particular prospect. Before I describe how to conduct the customer needs analysis, I want you to understand what life is like on the buyer's side of the desk. You'll quickly grasp why it is so important to use this step to listen more than you talk. The customer needs analysis is about your prospect's problems and needs and not yours.

Professional buyers meet with salespeople all the time. Imagine if you were on the other side of the desk from salespeople all day. What would you want out of those meetings? Well, one buyer created an ideal sales call from her perspective.

The Prospect's Plea

To: All Sales Representatives
From: Ellen Armstrong
Subject: Conditions for Seeing Me

You have requested some of my valuable time. I understand that it is your job. But please understand that if I saw every rep who requested an appointment, it would leave me no time to deal with my other responsibilities. I may agree to see you if you adhere to the following guidelines:

- Do not attempt to sell me anything until you understand my needs, challenges, and past experiences.

- Do not pressure me into doing business with you. The more you push, the less I will respond.

- Don't demean and criticize your competitors. If you do, I will ask you to leave. I don't mind if you make valid comparisons. Gossip, however, contributes nothing of value to my business.

- Be clear, concise, and articulate. If I agree to see you, I expect you to describe with the highest degree of professionalism how your product will benefit my business. If you ramble, you will lose my attention.

- I prefer ideas rather than programs. Be prepared to offer me your best ideas and opportunities. Programs that give me a "good deal" on products that don't best fit my needs tend to work better for you than for me. Show me plans that you would buy if you were me.

- Be a resource. Learn about my business and show me that you care. You can't get results for me if you don't know what's going on in my world.

- Listen as much as you talk, and don't waste my time.

Now you have my conditions for an appointment. Please sign it and mail it back to me. Then, call again and I will consider giving you my valuable time.

Bestselling author and business guru Ken Blanchard once wrote, "If you can't describe the problem you're having [with a person] in behavior terms, you don't have a problem, you're just complaining." The buyer's memo to all sales representatives describes—in behavioral terms—the behavior she expects, as well as the behavior that will cause vendors to lose style points (and the sale) with her. Her plea to the vendors who call on her is for them to take their selling efforts to the next level. She doesn't have The Chart or use the term "Level 1," but she clearly is fed up with the number of Level 1 salespeople she is seeing and the quality of the meetings they are having. She clearly describes the Level 2 behavior she prefers, and even suggests that people have Level 3 "moments" with her (e.g., "Be a resource").

Buyers want to be engaged. They want new ideas and outside perspective. They want to work with the best salespeople. If you believe, as I do, that most buyers would say, "Do not attempt to sell me anything until you understand my needs, challenges, and past experiences," then doing a customer needs analysis is the logical next step in the sales process.

The Customer Needs Analysis

The purpose of the customer needs analysis (step 12) is to understand the prospect's business better and business problems more deeply. That puts you in position to make better recommendations.

Here is the critical step every accidental salesperson skips: Before you start firing questions at the prospect, take time to sell the prospect on the benefits of answering the questions and going through your consultative process.

Consultative selling is still the norm. Neil Rackham's *SPIN Selling* was a breakthrough book when first published in 1988 that documented Rackham's research into what top sales performers do differently than moderate performers. His conclusion is that top performers ask better questions.

That said, you should never ask questions to which the answers are readily available in a couple of mouse clicks. When I was a very young salesperson, I used a four-page "Consultant Sell" form. Because I was selling advertising, one of the questions on the form was, "What are your store hours?" One day, I asked a successful, hard-driving retailer that question. I'll never forget his answer, nor did I ever ask that question again.

"It's on the door," was all he said.

There is no doubt that asking good questions will help you. You'll gain valuable information with which to sell more of your product.

But how will answering your questions benefit the prospect? Answer that before you start asking questions and the quality of the answers you get will be much better.

You've done everything right up to this point. You have described your process to the prospect. He understands and has bought the way you sell. You are very close to being in position to propose what you sell, but you need to know more.

Begin your customer needs analysis with the prospect by laying out both your rationale for doing so and the benefits of asking these questions. Back in Chapter 2, I told the story about the car dealer who canceled his advertising. He demanded to meet with all of the media representatives for twenty minutes each in one day. He told me that it was the most boring day of his life. When I presented the benefit of getting an intelligent proposal, he was more than happy to invest an hour and a half with me instead of twenty minutes. An intelligent proposal may or may not be a strong enough benefit for your prospect, but it's a start.

On the other hand, you may want to whip out a copy of The Chart and do a little self-disclosure. For instance:

> I got into sales accidentally, but I sell on purpose. I want to create customers instead of make sales. By going through this process and answering my questions, you'll gain some new insights because I'll ask some questions for free that you'd pay a consultant to ask you. I'll be in a position to customize a solution instead of having to guess at what you might need. Fair enough?

Don't try to hide what's happening and slide into your consultation. If you want the prospect to disclose more information, you have to disclose some information, too. Making that one refinement will differentiate you and put one more point in your credibility column.

Your company may require that a questionnaire be filled out. Fill out as much of it as you can before you meet with the prospect. You may need technical information in order to engineer a solution, so I'm going to give you a wonderfully simple, all-purpose customer needs analysis approach that will enhance whatever you are doing now. Here's how I first learned about it.

ACCIDENTAL SALES TRAINING SEMINAR

The "Communications" Salesperson

I'm a sales trainer, but I'm also a buyer. I had agreed to sit down with Jeff, a salesperson who sold office telephone systems. He was in our conference room to find out if he could get our telephone business. I wasn't impressed with his opening.

"You have a beautiful office," said Jeff.

"Jeff, you know I'm a sales trainer. Don't do the beautiful office opening."

"Seriously," he said, "we're a multibillion-dollar company and your office is nicer than our Madison office. Just an observation."

"Thanks," I said. Then he impressed me.

"Chris, we want to do more than sell cheap long-distance rates. We want to offer communication solutions. In order for me to see the business from your perspective, I'd like to do a quick force-field analysis."

(Good job of explaining why he was doing a force-field analysis, I observed, but what, I wondered, is a force-field analysis?)

Jeff took a legal pad and drew a line at the bottom. "Let's go back to Day 1," he said, and he wrote "Day 1" next to the line. "Day 1 was when?"

"Well, Sarah and I founded this company in January 1983."

"Okay." He continued talking as he drew another line above the bottom line and wrote "Today" next to it. "From 1983 until today, you have done a lot of things to get you to this level of success." As Jeff said that, he drew four arrows from the Day 1 line pointing upward to the Today line.

All I can tell you is that each one of those arrows elicited a response from me. With no further questions, I was labeling the arrows and Jeff took notes. Those arrows made me talk, and I gave him specific information about our philosophy, our business practices, and our strengths as a company.

When I'd labeled all the arrows and was starting to run out of steam, he took the piece of paper and added a line at the top. "Let's call this line the next level. It's the next level of growth or the dream you have for improving your business. What is keeping you from getting there?" Jeff asked.

With that, he drew four arrows from the top line to the Today line. It was obvious that these were the forces holding us back, and I ranted for ten minutes about my competition, the cost of marketing, and several other problems.

Jeff had gained some valuable insights into our business, and I had experienced a new kind of consultation that worked so well, I immediately started teaching it in my seminars. Once again I had learned about something useful in another accidental sales seminar.

The force-field analysis, I later learned, was originally developed by Kurt Lewin, founder of the National Training Laboratories, to facilitate team building. I encountered it again when I attended a lab on facilitation for professional speakers put on by the National Speakers Association. Consultants learn how to use force-field analysis as a facilitation tool. If you want to come across as more of a consultative salesperson than a product-focused vendor, then use the method consultants use.

The force-field analysis doesn't really require a form. It works better when you draw it on a whiteboard, legal pad, or place mat at a restaurant. One salesperson told us about doing a force-field analysis on the back of a golf scorecard while he and the prospect were playing a round of golf.

The next time you need to gain more information, play around with this method. The force-field analysis works very well when you are presenting it to a committee. You will get many different opinions about what the arrows mean, and you can factor that into your proposal to the committee.

Once your prospect has labeled the arrows, you ask more specific questions to get at the data you need. Some salespeople know how to ask questions and some don't. Notice the difference between these two approaches, both of which go after the same data.

Example 1

"So, what is your budget?" the accidental salesperson asks.

"That's confidential information," the client replies guardedly.

Example 2

"In order for me to make an intelligent proposal, I need to know your budget," says the accidental salesperson.

"Oh, of course. It's $123,000," the cooperative prospect responds.

In example 2, the salesperson gives the prospect a benefit (intelligent proposal) for providing the information. This example doesn't even look or sound like a question. It's called an embedded question. Read it again.

"In order for me to make an intelligent proposal,
I need to know your budget."

The question doesn't begin with who, what, when, where, why, or how. It doesn't end with a question mark. The question (What's your budget, anyway?) is embedded in the statement. You may have used embedded questions accidentally in the past. Use them on purpose and your needs analysis meetings will be discussions instead of interrogations. Here are several more examples of embedded questions:

"I'd be interested in learning about your criteria for making the change."

"Give me more information about the area that is giving you the most trouble."

"I am wondering if you have tried to solve this problem internally."

"I want to understand the decision-making process you are going through."

"Talk about how this idea might improve your operation."

"Tell me more about the problems you've had in the past with this kind of equipment."

Gathering data and assessing prospects' needs is a process. Too often salespeople go through the motions of filling out the questionnaires so that they can go right to their presentation. When you are selling on purpose, your mindset is that every prospect interaction is an opportunity to gain more information and qualify the prospect better. Once the prospect becomes a customer, the data gathering continues. The situation is always changing.

Today, of course, your prospects want you to come to the table knowing the answers to the questions they used to have time to sit down and answer. They are too pressed for time to teach you things you can learn yourself by consulting a website. That is why premeeting preparation is so important. It immediately differentiates you as the salesperson who does his or her homework.

Accidental Salesperson Axiom:
Asking questions is the answer to most sales problems.

Corollary:
If you listen more than you talk, you will seem even more intelligent than you are.

Sales trainers talk about listening until they are blue in the face. Maybe that's the problem: We *talk* about listening. Virtually every salesperson has been told to ask questions and listen more. I have heard it said that a good consultant should have gray hair and hemorrhoids. The gray hair makes you look distinguished. The hemorrhoids make you look concerned.

That's the essence of consulting. You are more concerned about the process than the outcome. You don't get ahead of yourself and rush to the pitch and pricing. You ask questions and listen. You seek first to understand instead of being understood, as Stephen Covey, author of *The 7 Habits of Highly Effective People*, so beautifully put it.

When you really care about getting a result for your customer instead of just another sale for you, the customer can sense it.

When you are curious and interested, you'll find that you get stories from the prospect rather than just dry facts. When prospects tell you their stories and engage you, they become emotionally involved in the process. They go beyond the facts and give you more inside, behind-the-scenes information. Instead of moving quickly through your list of questions, take the time to ask follow-up questions and get the stories behind the facts.

You must really want to know the answers to the questions you are asking. Too many salespeople simply feign listening while waiting until it's their turn to talk.

Every time you meet with the prospect, you have an opportunity to update your database and discover more problems you can help solve. Qualifying is part of step 12 in your sales process. You need to ask more questions in order to make an intelligent presentation.

Old-school sales trainers harangued their audiences with the acronym A-B-C. "Always Be Closing," they said. In today's sales environment, it might be more appropriate to leave you with a new acronym: N-Q-Q. Never Quit Qualifying.

Booking Your Proposal Meeting

Once you have qualified the prospect and have determined there is a problem you can solve, book the meeting to present the formal proposal (step 13). Don't leave the needs analysis meeting without an appointment.

One of the biggest mistakes accidental salespeople make is waiting until they have the proposal written before they book the appointment to present it. Once you book the proposal appointment you can't procrastinate. You have a compelling deadline that propels your proposal writing. (With the proposal-writing template in the next chapter, you'll easily meet that deadline.)

Depending on how long and involved your proposals are, you may want to limit the number of needs analysis interviews. For example, if you have done two needs analysis interviews, don't do another one until you have converted one of the interviews into a proposal. Then allow yourself one more interview. Proposal meetings are where you make your money. You may love having dozens of interested prospects. But until you write and present a proposal, asking prospects to invest real money, you'll never know how interested they really are.

Of course, not every proposal has to be written down and have ten PowerPoint slides and an implementation schedule. You may be selling a relatively straightforward product that the buyer wants. If you do, you can skip steps 14 and 15 (writing your proposal and making your presentation, respectively) and go right to step 16 and close the sale. Here's how I handled such a situation.

Four Words You Don't Want to Hear

"Send me a proposal."

Those are the four words I don't want to hear. You don't, either. They are four words I have come to dread. You have now lengthened the selling cycle and added two or three hours of work to your day. That's if you write your own proposals. If you work for a larger company, where proposals have to come out of the marketing department or from the sales secretary, then you have an even longer wait until the proposal is ready to send over (or take back) to the prospect.

Too many salespeople hear those words and think they are a buying signal. When I hear them I think, "Boy, I must have done a lousy job of demonstrating what our offering can do if the prospect wants it in writing."

Asking for something in writing is almost a conditioned response for a buyer. You can react to the request by dutifully going back and writing a proposal, or you can ask a few more questions.

Here's an actual conversation I had with a prospect who was thinking about buying some sales training:

PROSPECT: Send me a proposal.

ME: When you say "proposal," what would you like it to have in it?

PROSPECT: I just need you to document what you are going to deliver and how much it costs.

ME: Is it a document you need to take to your CFO to get a check cut, or do you need it to help you to do some more selling internally?

PROSPECT: No, just to take to our CFO.

ME: Then you really need an invoice with units, pricing, and terms, right?

PROSPECT: That will work.

ME: When would you like it dated for implementation?

PROSPECT: A week from now, when we get into the third quarter.

ME: Done. Thank you for the order.

PROSPECT: I'm looking forward to working with you, Chris.

It is much easier to write an invoice than to write a proposal with rationale and specs. While I was able to skip writing and delivering the proposal, during this discussion I was still conducting a customer needs analysis in order to close the deal.

Selling is hard enough without making extra work for yourself.

The simpler the sale, the less you need a long written proposal. If the product you are selling requires no customization and isn't an engineered solution, you can simply say, "I brought an order form. Do you need more documentation than that?"

However, if you find yourself having to write and deliver more complex presentations, you'll get plenty of help with that in the next two chapters.

CHAPTER 10

Writing Your Proposal: Step 14

It's time to take the mystery and misery out of proposal writing. Using the proposal-writing template in this chapter as your guide, you will soon be including Level 2, 3, and 4 pages in your proposals. This one refinement automatically makes every proposal you write and present more client-focused. You'll learn how to plug into a powerful formula found in an obvious but overlooked source—any infomercial on television. Along the way, you will learn to ask your prospects to help you put together their proposal. By making a "preliminary proposal" you can get feedback that makes your "final proposal" more client-focused and, thus, more likely to be approved.

I always assume that my readers and my seminar participants are doing most things right when selling. Even if you do 90 percent to 95 percent of everything right, I promise you that making just a few of the refinements suggested in this chapter will immediately differentiate your written proposal from those of your competition.

Grading Your Past and Future Proposals

There is an interesting story behind the proposal-writing template. Years ago, a major Canadian broadcaster retained me to do some management training. The goal was to create nationwide standards of performance for various sales teams. The company wanted to be able to judge a salesperson in Moose Jaw, Saskatchewan, by the same standards as a salesperson in Toronto, Ontario. The broadcasting company was looking for objective ways to identify "good" performance in order to train everyone in the organization to that standard.

A standard is a measurable indicator of performance, often involving a consequence. In the past, most standards for salespeople involved quantity instead of quality. The Chart changes some of that. You still have to develop a certain number of proposals, but writing five Level 2 proposals of higher quality may result in more sales than writing ten Level 1 proposals of lower quality. That is so obvious that even old-school sales managers buy the logic of it.

The problem has been measuring the quality of a proposal before you present it. The proposal-writing template solves that problem.

In preparing for the management training session, I requested and received copies of real proposals the company's salespeople had already written. Unfortunately, by the time the proposals stopped arriving at our offices, I had more than a thousand pages of reading to do to prepare for the upcoming manager's meeting. I actually lugged these proposals from city to city as I conducted other seminars. But, at the end of the each day, I felt too tired to attack the intimidating stack of papers. Even though the weight of those papers in my suitcase was nearly enough to pull my shoulder from its socket, the proposals remained unread until the day before the management training seminar. However, in this case, procrastination proved to be a good thing.

On my way to Winnipeg, where the meeting was being held, I had a three-hour layover at O'Hare International Airport and headed for the Red Carpet Club. After settling in, I read three appalling proposals in rapid succession. There were eighty more to look at. After skimming the next half dozen, I quit reading. *Why should I be reading these?* I thought. *The managers ought to be experiencing these boring, company-focused proposals the same way I am. They should understand how bad these proposals really are.* I couldn't just tell them. So I designed an exercise.

In Winnipeg, I passed out copies of The Chart to each sales manager. They found it easy enough to talk about the levels at which different salespeople on their teams were operating.

Then I suggested that if salespeople can have measurable Level 1, 2, 3, and 4 "moments" with their prospects, it might also be possible to measure Level 1, 2, 3, and 4 pages or sections in their proposals. For example, a page about a prospect's problem would be Level 2, a printout of various rates or product specs the salespeople were trying to sell would be Level 1, and so on. I had them use The Chart to grade each page of the proposal: 1, 2, 3, or 4. They added the scores and divided that score by the number of proposal pages.

Working in pairs, the managers graded proposals their team members had turned out, as well as proposals their partner's team members had written. There were audible groans as they read and graded. The mood in the room was somber.

"My people are cranking out crap, eh?" one of the managers said. "And they're taking the trouble to put a color cover page on it and bind it before they give it to a prospect."

"There was nothing in here about the client," observed another. "It was a pure Level 1 proposal from a person I thought was operating at a much higher level."

Their salespeople were not trying to turn out bad presentations. They just did not have a model for what "good" looked like, so they had "defaulted" to Level 1.

There are days when I learn as much from the audience as they learn from me. By the end of this management training seminar, we had made a major breakthrough: There are no pure Level 4 salespeople and there can never be a pure Level 4 proposal. Level 2 became the standard of what "good" looks like in the company. Level 2 proposals were 100 percent better than the Level 1 proposals they were turning out.

The story doesn't end there. For the next three years we worked with this client and others to set down the criteria to measure the different types of pages we found in proposals. The proposal-writing template is the result.

Using the Proposal-Writing Template

The proposal-writing template in Figure 10-1 lets you check the quality of your proposal before you present it. You can use specific suggestions for Level 3 and Level 4 pages by going through the checklists. The idea is not to make a thirty-page proposal but to make sure that, even if your proposal is five pages, it has higher-level pages (or sections) before the unavoidable Level 1 material. I say "unavoidable" because you have to discuss price and product specifications. These materials should follow higher-level pages, however, and not lead off your proposal.

Until you've established that the prospect has a problem and offered proof that your product is the solution, the price and specifications aren't really relevant.

The best thing you can do right now is to stop reading this book and grade some of the proposals you have written to see exactly what level you've attained. Then set a goal for taking your next proposal to a higher level. Be brutally honest with yourself. If it's a close call, grade yourself on the low side.

Look at all the Level 1 possibilities:

- Spec sheets
- Price lists
- Catalogs
- Brochures
- One-sheeters about products
- Company press releases
- Pictures of your plant or operation

These are the things accidental salespeople automatically reach for as "filler" to bulk up their proposals. They mistakenly believe that their expensive brochures and reams of product literature are important sales tools. After all, their companies have shelving units straining beneath the weight of all the expensive four-color printing. Let's get these pictures of our product into the hands of our prospects, thinks the accidental salesperson.

Figure 10-1 Add quality to every proposal by including Level 2, 3, and 4 pages along with your Level 1 material.

Proposal-Writing Template

Level 1 Pages
❏ Spec sheets
❏ Price lists
❏ Catalog
❏ Brochure
❏ One-sheeters about products
❏ Company press release
❏ Pictures of your plant or operation

Level 2 Pages
❏ A cover page that offers a solution to a problem
❏ A business balance sheet
❏ A problem description page
❏ A problem solution page that shows how your product or service addresses the prospect's need
❏ Testimonial letters from your satisfied customers

	Level 1 Account Executive	Level 2 Salesperson or Problem Solver	Level 3 Professional Salesperson	Level 4 Sales and Marketing Professional
Level of trust	Neutral or distrustful	Some credibility	Credible to highly credible; based on salesperson's history	Complete trust based on established relationships and past performance
Goal/call objective	To open doors; to "see what's going on"	To persuade and make a sale or to advance the prospect through the process	Customer creation and retention; to "find the fit"; to upgrade the client and gain more information	To continue upgrading and increase share of business
Approach and involvement	Minimal or nonexistent	Well-planned; work to get prospect to buy into the process	True source of industry information and "business intelligence"	Less formal and more comfortable because of trust and history
Concern or self-esteem issue	Being liked	Being of service, solving a problem	Being a resource	Being an "outside insider"
Precall preparation	Memorize a canned pitch or "wing it"	Set call objectives; prescript questions; articulate purpose–process–payoff	Research trade magazines, Internet; analyze client's competition	Thorough preparation, sometimes with proprietary information unavailable to other reps
Presentation	Product literature, spec sheets, rate sheets	Product solution for problem they uncover during needs analysis	Systems solutions	Return on investment proof and profit improvement strategies
Point of contact	Buyer or purchasing agent	End users as well as buyer or purchasing agent	Buyers, end users, and an "internal coach" or advocate within client's company	"Networked" through the company; may be doing business in multiple divisions

DEFAULT   ▲   PREFERENCE SETTINGS

Level 3 Pages
❏ Facts from the client's annual report or Web site
❏ Facts from industry trade publications
❏ Facts from Internet searches
❏ Facts from business publications
❏ Quotes from business experts
❏ Information on the client's competition that relates to your recommendation
❏ Industry research

Level 4 Pages
❏ Research on the client's customer
❏ Focus group information
❏ Consumer research
❏ Recommendations that affect cost savings, efficiency, and profit enhancements

Lead with Level 3 and 4 pages.

Calculate your score according to this formula: Total points scored on all pages (   ) divided by number of pages in proposal (   ) equals average score of proposal (   ).

In reality, these Level I pages drag down proposal quality. They make a proposal more about the product than about the prospect's problem.

The proposal-writing template prompts you to consider a variety of higher-level pages or sections. Don't feel you have to have a page for everything in every box. Having three or four client-focused pages is a good thing. If I hit my prospect's website and find the company's mission includes training and developing its people, you can bet it will appear in one of the first two pages of my proposal. Starting with a Level 3 page that positions my services as a natural extension of the mission adds power.

Great proposals are almost as easy to produce as poor ones using the proposal-writing template. You'll soon discover that it's easier to close prospects on higher-level proposals, too.

Wanted: Shorter Proposals

The average length of the eighty proposals I was lugging around in my suitcase was twenty pages. That's way too long for today's rapidly paced world.

A successful magazine publisher once asked me to conduct focus groups with the magazine's advertisers regarding proposal length and content. More than forty advertisers participated in three ninety-minute sessions. We sat around a table with a digital audio recorder turned on while I asked questions about the magazine's sales reps calling on them and whether their proposals were on target.

"What does good look like in a written proposal?" I asked.

The consensus was that "concise" is good. "Edit" and "summarize" were words that came up as well, as did "cut to the chase."

"If we're at the proposal phase, we don't need twenty pages on the product or the company history. We know all of that already," said one buyer. "We have to extract the two relevant pages of your proposal and paste them into a new document."

Check the length of your last few proposals. What words, pages, or sections could you have eliminated? How long did it take you to get to the point? If your customers demanded a one-page proposal, what vital information would have made the cut?

Mark Twain wrote, "I didn't have time to write a short letter, so I wrote a long one instead." It takes time to edit yourself.

Time-starved prospects may see your conciseness as a positive point of difference. And your proposal will get read while longer ones clog virtual and physical in-boxes. Here's what I know for sure: Your proposals are too long and take too much time to write. I know this because most of us equate length with thoroughness. And thoroughness means long, boring presentations.

But don't take my word for it. Silicon Valley venture capitalist and bestselling author Guy Kawasaki says that any presentation should follow his 10-20-30 Rule: It should be 10 pages long, last 20 minutes, and use 30-point type. If you have an hour set aside for the meeting, you can then have a 40-minute conversation about the details of the proposal instead of filling up the whole hour.

I like simple, easy-to-follow rules and formulas like Kawasaki's. But do your own research. Ask your customers the same question I asked the Canadian buyers: What does good look like to you in a written proposal from a salesperson?

When someone asks you to put it in writing, you have every right to ask any or all of the following questions:

- What format (e.g., PowerPoint, a Word document, a spreadsheet) is easiest to work with?

- How long do you want it to be?

- What don't you need in a proposal?

- What points do you want clarified?

- Do you want my fancy folder or a quick-and-dirty outline so that you can have it promptly?

- What's my deadline?

- What happens once you have the proposal in hand?

With the answer to some of those questions in your notes, you can return to the proposal-writing template and create your preliminary proposal. See if you don't save yourself a lot of time.

Preliminary Proposals Take the Pressure Off

The trouble with most proposals is that they are yours instead of the prospect's. You might want to ask the prospect if you can put together a preliminary proposal to run by him informally to get some feedback and guidance.

The preliminary proposal is an opportunity to present your recommendations without the pressure of asking for the order. By sharing the ideas you plan to present more formally later, you allow the prospect to give you reactions and input.

As an added bonus, you might find that, with a few added bullets and some sentences your prospect inserted, the preliminary proposal quickly becomes the final proposal.

Proposals Are Part of the Price of Success

Some salespeople resist written proposals. One seminar participant put it this way: "Chris, what if I go to all this work and the prospect doesn't buy? I will have put in a lot of hours for nothing."

Obviously, you only do proposals for qualified prospects. Still, there will always be a certain amount of uncertainty in selling. One sure thing, though: To be successful, you are going to have to do a lot of work up front for free, hoping that the prospect will pay you later.

Accidental Salesperson Axiom:
Doing the work before you get paid for
it is part of the price of success.

Corollary:
You may put in an honest day's work and
not get an honest day's pay.

If you work on straight commission, you prospect for free. You do a customer needs analysis for free. You do the research for free. Then you write the proposal for free. Even when your company pays you a salary or a draw, the client pays you only after you've written a good proposal.

That's the way it works.

At least you don't have to pay to make your presentation to the prospect.

What if you did have to pay to make your presentation? Think about that for a moment. You obviously would put more time and thought into it. You probably would even rehearse it a few times. You would make certain your proposal flowed logically from your opening statement (or question) to the close. You'd make sure you proved each point you made. You'd demonstrate your product's superiority and offer testimonials. You would definitely ask for the order and you would not take the prospect's first "No" for an answer. You would review your key points and ask again, and make certain to combine logical arguments with emotional reasons to get the prospect to act *now* instead of later. Wouldn't you?

The Infomercial as Visual Sales Proposal

The structure of a TV infomercial offers a proven way to structure your written proposal. Think about it this way: TV commercials are thirty-second sales presentations. Extended to thirty minutes, these TV commercials become "infomercials," or long-form advertisements. The producers of infomercials pay hundreds of thousands of dollars to create and present their sales messages. They cannot afford to leave anything out or anything to chance. The next time you hit "Guide" on your remote and see "Paid Programming" instead of the name of a show, tune in for half an hour. Don't write down the toll-free number. Rather, take notes on how the advertiser puts together the sales presentation. Then go and do likewise.

One morning I sat down and watched one infomercial after another and took notes, just like I'm suggesting you do. Of course, by now I could be making millions buying real estate with no money down. I could have reshaped my body with the latest $99 Ab

Trainer. But, no. I haven't even applied the revolutionary protectant to preserve the paint on my car. I'm still here, trying to help you put together more powerful presentations.

Every infomercial follows this basic three-step formula:

1. Set forth the problem.
2. Explain the solution.
3. Demonstrate how your product or service best provides the solution.

The late infomercial pioneer Alvin Eicoff described the process in his book, *Successful Broadcast Advertising*. The impact Eicoff made on his industry is so great that *Time* magazine published his obituary when he died in 2002.

Every infomercial begins with a Level 2 "moment." The headline speaks directly to the audience about their problems—not the product. An infomercial for a course on buying real estate with no money down opens with a real person talking about retirement. He says, "For most people when they retire, their home is their saving grace. They sell their big home and buy a smaller one. They invest the difference and live off it. But what if they had five homes?"

The product is the solution to the problem being presented. But you still don't see the real estate course itself. First, you see real people who already have benefited from the course. In these testimonials, people talk about other programs they have tried and explain why this course was the answer to their prayers.

When the infomercial sells an exercise program, people talk about other programs they have tried and why this one is better. Ultimately, the inventor of the product or developer of the program comes on and tells the story of how he discovered an amazing secret and how thrilled he is that he can make the world a better place. The storytelling adds credibility and makes the audience feel connected to the people behind the product.

The advertiser explains the solution and then demonstrates exactly how the product provides the solution. The demonstrations in infomercials offer evidence. Exercise and diet programs use "before" pictures of very heavy people and then have the transformed people walk on camera.

All that's left is to ask for the order. "Get out your pen," commands the announcer, "here comes that toll-free number." The announcer summarizes the problem, explains the solution, reminds you of the amazing demonstrations you've just seen, presents the product and the pricing options, and asks you to act now.

Not everyone does. But enough people do. Guthy-Renker, one of the top direct marketing companies in the world, alone does $1.8 billion in annual sales. If you want to get better at writing proposals, pay attention to ads for Tony Robbins's *Ultimate Edge* CDs and Susan Lucci's Youthful Essence skin-care system.

"But wait, there's still more."

There's always more in infomercials. Most infomercials raise objections that the prospect may be having and answer them before the prospect asks. This is a powerful technique. If you raise the objection first, the prospect is less likely to use it later.

Infomercials also make it clear that the buyer won't be alone. Thousands (even millions) of people have already turned their lives around with this product.

Infomercials compare the price of the product to something completely different. "This course costs less than dinner for two at a nice restaurant." This is a technique that gets people to think about things they have already purchased instead of comparing the product with a competing product.

Infomercials always make the product part of a "complete system" by adding a booklet, a video, or a bottle of some other kind of cleaner or solvent. There is nothing left to buy. You get the complete system for two easy payments.

And finally, there is always a money-back guarantee if the customer is not completely satisfied. This is called "risk reversal." It makes it easier for the prospect to give the product a try. You may not be able to offer a money-back guarantee, but the more you can do to assure the prospect there is very little risk, the easier it will be to make the sale.

People who produce and place infomercials pay for the privilege of presenting. They are giving you a free seminar on how to sell. Ignore the lessons at your own risk.

There is plenty of structure to follow by combining the three-part formula for writing an infomercial and the components suggested in the proposal-writing template. You'll find that you start gathering data immediately to fit your proposal-writing format.

One thing I urge you to start doing right away is to put the problem on the cover page. For example:

How to Eliminate 7 Hours of Costly Downtime per Month

or

How to Transform Your Sales Department into a Sales Force

It is tempting—but completely unnecessary—to put your company's logo and your name on the cover page. Set forth the problem and you start your proposal with a Level 2 page. Then add pages that explain why your solution is best. *Demonstrate* how your product provides the best solution. *Detail* exactly what the prospect gets and when. And ask for the order.

Written proposals can help you sell, but they shouldn't be asked to sell for you. Think of the proposal as a visual aid instead of a term paper. Your written proposal is just the outline. You provide the details in conversation. There is a terrible tendency today for salespeople to overuse PowerPoint presentations and similar tools. They make too many slides and then read them to the prospect. Bad move.

Watch out for one other thing. With bound proposals, bored prospects can read ahead to the investment page and start poring over the specifics instead of considering your rationale and weighing your evidence first.

You control the focus of the presentation by controlling how much information you give the prospect at the outset of your meeting. Handing the prospect one page of your proposal at a time lets you control the flow of information. Get feedback on that one page. Then move on to the next one.

Finally, work on your stories. Spreadsheets make it possible to add page after page of mind-numbing figures to your presentation. Stories add emotion and passion to the evidence you present. You need to present logical and emotional reasons for the prospect to buy.

Now all you have to do is execute.

To make execution even easier, I have put a copy of my Proposal Producer at TheAccidentalSalesperson2012.com for you to download. The Proposal Producer incorporates the advice in this chapter and walks you through the key elements of any presentation. You simply fill in the blanks with your data to quickly produce a concise, client-focused written proposal. The Proposal Producer prompts you to create your cover page with a headline that offers a benefit or savings to the customer. On the next page, you bullet-point your understanding of the problem, pain, or issue. On subsequent pages, you make the business case for your solution; make specific recommendations; lay out the pricing and terms; and, if it's a complicated installation, provide an implementation calendar.

But all you've done so far is write the proposal. You've got to deliver it (step 15). The next chapter shows you how to stand up and sell it.

CHAPTER 11

Making Your Presentation Like a Pro: Step 15

At one point in my life, I thought about being a stand-up comedian.

But I didn't want to work nights.

So I became a professional speaker and got to work long days instead. I have conducted more than 2,100 sales and sales management seminars and have learned a lot about how to connect with an audience and hold people's attention for up to six hours a day.

In this chapter, I want to share some of my speaking "secrets" with you. You don't have to have a large audience to use my ideas. I once did a seminar with two people in it. And I was one of them! The same principles apply.

You have already completed the other fourteen steps in the sales process. Here's how to make the most out of step 15, making your presentation.

The Three Essential Elements to Manage in a Presentation

There are seminars for people who conduct seminars. And I have been to quite a few of them. I was fortunate enough to learn early in my speaking career that there are three elements that you must manage when making a presentation:

1. The Content

2. The Process

3. The Environment

Let's consider each of these separately.

The *content* is what you are trying to get across. It is the proposal you've written in step 14, coupled with the way you deliver it. It's what you say, how you say it, and the collateral materials you use to convey it. And it can take many forms, including stories, video testimonials, price sheets, spec sheets, PowerPoint slides, web tours, and audience feedback.

In communicating your content, you want to transfer emotion as well as impart information. Your belief in what you are proposing must ignite your passion. You also want to make your presentation a dialogue rather than a monologue. Two-way presentations are easier on both you and the prospect.

You have written the proposal, but your presentation is not about reading it. You could attach your PowerPoint slides to an e-mail and let your prospect read it. Your presence makes your presentation more passionate and persuasive. At least it should.

You will be more persuasive when you give off these three vibes:

1. I'm glad to be here.

2. I know what I'm talking about.

3. I love what I'm doing.

If I was in the room when you were making your sales presentation, would I see you standing tall, speaking with confidence, smiling, making eye contact, and being totally present and there for the customer? If you are worried about making the sale, or if you are afraid of getting up in front of people, it will show.

Would I see you reading from your slides or else putting up a slide, letting your prospect read it, and then adding an anecdote? If so, let me suggest that instead you put up a slide with a small amount of content, and let your prospect read it, and then embellish from there with your anecdote. Or you could simply ask the prospect what her initial reaction was as you gently gestured toward the screen.

I have been asked if I get nervous before making a presentation. I can honestly answer, "I am nervous when I am not making a presentation, because that means I'm *not* making an income."

That said, rehearsing your presentation is the best way I know to gain confidence quickly. The first person who hears a major presentation should not be the prospect.

The *process* is how you and the prospect are working together. Is the atmosphere tense or laid-back? Is the prospect collaborative or combative?

Here's how you go about managing the process: You stop delivering your content and you make a comment about the way you and the prospect are working together. A positive process comment might be, "You seemed more interested (or excited) when we were going over that last feature." A negative comment might be, "You seem distracted. Did I lose you somewhere?"

This is not psychotherapy. It's simply taking the prospect's temperature instead of simply plodding forward with your presentation. When you sense the presentation is not going well, you need to stop it right there and work with your prospect to get it back on track. You may even have to abandon your written presentation and improvise based on the feedback you are getting. Most salespeople don't even know they are allowed to make a process comment. Or they are too afraid to comment that the meeting is not going well and instead rush through their content without stopping to resolve any problems they and their prospect are having in working together.

Finally, the *environment* is the combination of all the subtle factors that can help to make a presentation a success or drag it down and make it a failure. These factors include the room, the lighting, the temperature, and the length of the meeting. Environment is extremely important to the energy of the meeting and its outcome. To the extent you can manage the environment, you can become a much more professional and effective presenter. It is easier to manage the delivery of the content and the process when you aren't hemmed in by a cramped room or forced to do without the visual aids you need to enhance your presentation.

As a professional speaker, I manage the environment of my presentation by arriving seventy-five to ninety minutes early to make sure the room is set up the way I want it. I like an aisle down the middle of the room so that I can walk into the audience. I want the screen angled and off to one side of the room so that I am not walking in front of my slide projector. I want round tables so that group discussion can occur at vital parts of the session. My assistant sends a diagram of the ideal room setup, plus a checklist of audio-visual requirements, to the sales department of the hotel where I'll be speaking. The checklist helps me manage the environment as much as I can before I even arrive so that I can focus on my presentation. The fewer the surprises, the easier it is to concentrate on delivering my content and managing the process.

Another aspect of managing your presentation is asking to meet in a conference room instead of meeting in the prospect's office and having to make your presentation across her big desk. Delivering your presentation on "neutral ground" changes the dynamic of the meeting. If you get a conference room, you can arrive ten to fifteen minutes early to get set up and settled in. Use that time to ask for a glass of water, pass out an agenda for each meeting participant, and make sure that the lights are on and the screen is behind you.

It's Your Presentation; Make It Your Room, Too

I once accompanied a salesperson on a call. He had requested the meeting be held in the conference room. So far, so good. But when we got there, the projector was at the far end of the table. With little time before the presentation was to begin, he connected his computer to the projector and took his position at that end of the table. The problem was that the *screen* was on the opposite end of the room, so when he put up his first slide the members of the buying committee were forced to turn their backs on him in order to see the presentation. As soon as he turned on the PowerPoint, he lost his ability to maintain eye contact and therefore lost control of the meeting. He droned on, addressing the back of their heads for nearly forty minutes and never got a second meeting.

Arriving earlier would have allowed him to reset the conference room, and carrying a cheap remote control slide changer would have enabled him to plug his computer in to the projector and take his place at the other end of the conference table, where he could look the members of the buying committee in the eye as they viewed the slides over his shoulder.

Environment matters. A lot.

I have made the same presentation four times in the same week in four different locations. The color of the carpet matters. The wattage of the lightbulbs matters. Whether there are windows with natural light pouring through them matters. A dimly lit room with multipurpose carpeting that hides food stains in its multicolored tufts can deaden the energy of speaker and audience members. The joke that killed yesterday falls flat or gets only a polite chuckle in a bad environment. Natural light energizes the audience and the presenter.

You can, and must, manage the content, the process, and the environment. To the extent that you are aware of these factors and bold enough to take charge, you will be a markedly more effective presenter.

Presentation Skills 101

I have seen salespeople who are nervous about making presentations. Not me. Like I said, I love getting up in front of an audience. Whether it's 300 people attending a six-hour seminar or a potential customer sitting across the desk, I can hardly wait to get started. The more you practice, the more you will enjoy making presentations.

At the same time, you have to practice using proven presentation principles. Here are my top seven.

Presentation Principle 1: Eye Contact Is a Powerful Connector

I like to look one audience member in the eye for about seven seconds and direct the presentation or speech to that one person. Then, I make eye contact with a person in the front row for seven seconds. After that, I'll turn to my right and make eye contact with someone ten rows back. It's an easy way to connect with people in the audience. It also helps manage your nerves because you are talking to one person at a time. When you are addressing a buying committee in a conference room, make sure you make eye contact with each person several times. It's a big mistake to talk only to the CEO or the person who invited you to the meeting. Make everyone feel included. Practice counting out seven seconds so that you get a sense for how long it is. Don't worry about counting seconds when you are actually doing the presentation. Trust yourself to spend about seven seconds with each person.

Presentation Principle 2: When Delivering the Punch Line or the Point of a Story, Deliver It to One Person

Early in my career I had an audience member who was studying improvisation. He gave me this very important feedback. "Chris, your eyes were flitting from person to person in the audience and it weakened your point," he said. I never forgot that lesson, and I started acting on it immediately. It works. Whenever you get a chance, watch professional speakers or even stand-up comics to see how they deliver their content.

Presentation Principle 3: Stand Up Whenever You Can

Don't assume a standing position to intimidate, but to demonstrate confidence that comes through in your body language. You can stand before a whiteboard and draw or write something on it. You can walk around the conference table and see how everyone's eyes follow you. You are your best visual aid. Gestures, posture, and movement add strength to any presentation.

Presentation Principle 4: Smile and Enjoy What You're Doing

It will make you much more engaging, and your audience will more easily relate to you and to what you are saying.

I once signed up for a "speakers' showcase." A speakers bureau charged me $750 to present twenty minutes of my material to sixty-five meeting planners in Philadelphia. There were three speakers an hour for five hours.

After my presentation, I left the stage and went out into the hallway of the hotel conference center. Another speaker participating in the showcase came up to me and said, "You looked like you were having fun up there."

"Anytime I pay $750 for twenty minutes, I'm going to do my best to enjoy it," I said. "Don't you love getting up in front of an audience?"

"I'm a college professor. I'm not nervous in front of my classes, but these people are 'corporate' and can pay me a lot more money than my college," he said.

"They won't pay you anything unless they enjoy your presentation. And if you're not enjoying your presentation, they won't enjoy it either," I said.

"I never thought about it that way," he admitted.

I offer you the same advice. Enjoy every minute of your presentation. Pour your energy into it and get energy back from the audience. Visualize how your presentation would go if your audience members were enjoying themselves, if they were thrilled to be spending the hour together instead of being back in their offices doing their boring jobs. Then let yourself do it.

Presentation Principle 5: Great Presentations Are Not Perfect Presentations

An acting coach once explained to me that stage fright is the fear of not giving a perfect performance. Once an actor accepts that there are no perfect performances and stops obsessing about having one, stage fright vanishes. They give great performances, not perfect ones. In the theater, an audience member's phone rings, another actor misses an entrance. The actor has to be in the moment and react to what's happening instead of worrying about making a mistake. In a sales presentation, the prospect asks you a tough question or your PowerPoint connection fails. So you improvise and move forward.

Presentation Principle 6: Understand That a Sales Presentation Is a Conversation, Not a Speech

And you shouldn't have to do all of the work or the talking. Getting feedback throughout your presentation is paramount. Think of it as closing every page or stage of your presentation.

You can elicit feedback and gauge interest all along by keeping prospects engaged. Before you change a slide or move to a new thought, ask one or two of the following questions:

- Does that make sense?
- Am I missing anything?
- What would you add?
- How close is this example to your situation?
- Are we together on that point?
- Do I understand your business?
- Have I restated your issues correctly?

You do have to provide information, demonstrate an understanding of the prospect's problems and business situation, and prove your capabilities. But the tendency is to tell too much and ask too little.

One thing that will telegraph your lack of experience and confidence is commenting on the fact that you are changing slides. Don't say, "On this next slide you will see . . ." Just change the damn slide.

Presentation Principle 7: When You Use Written
Sales Material, Don't Read It for Your Prospect

I've seen rookies and veterans hand a prospect a sheet of paper and then talk about it while the prospect tries to read it. I say "tries" because the prospect can't focus on reading when the sales rep is talking and can't listen to the rep while he's reading.

If you use written materials, hand over a page at a time. Be still as the prospect reads it. When the prospect's eyes meet yours, you can remain silent or raise an eyebrow as if to ask, "Well?" Or you can say, "What is your initial reaction?" Or "Does that information add value?"

It Gets Better

The more presentations you make, the better you get. You develop a sense of timing. You create your own shtick. You have customer success stories that you tell that make your point better than a spec sheet can.

Now that you have read about how to stand up and make better presentations, go out and apply one or two of these ideas in a real situation. Note what worked and what didn't. You will be a much stronger presenter the hundredth time than you will be the first time. But you have to start somewhere.

All that's left for you to do is to ask for the order (step 16).

You've earned it.

CHAPTER 12

"Closing" Is a Funny Word for It: Step 16

When you and the prospect have gone through the fifteen previous steps, you'll find yourself at the point where it's time to ask for the order. Step 16 is the "close." I put that word in quotation marks because I don't particularly like the connotations of the term.

You see, most closing problems aren't really closing problems. Too many accidental salespeople never get to the point in their sales process where closing is appropriate.

They don't keep their sales *open* long enough to get them closed.

Still, many sales managers fixate on closing to the exclusion of all the other steps in the process that make closing a "natural outcome" of taking prospects through your process.

My observation is that most sales managers need to impart a philosophy of closing to their sales teams rather than have them memorize a few surefire closing lines. I'm going to share with you my philosophy on closing, my system of beliefs and attitudes about closing. Here goes.

I believe that the word *closing* itself is not the best description of what salespeople do. The word carries the connotation of bringing something to an end. And while we *are* completing the sales process, we are only just starting the business relationship. There is no business relationship in my book until I have written someone a check or someone has written me a check and I have delivered a product or service.

Here are four new ways to think (philosophize) and speak about closing:

1. *Opening the Business Relationship.* Your prospect becomes your customer and writes you a check, and starts to enjoy the benefits of your product or service.

2. *Confirming the Order.* At this point, it's not a matter of a closing line, but simply a matter of the details of delivery dates. Once these details are worked out, there's nothing left to do but write the order.

3. *Implementing the Plan or Solution.* It's time to execute instead of talk. Implementation should be as exciting for the buyer as it is the seller. The buyer gets to solve her problem and improve her business.

4. *Acquiring the Order.* Gaining a new customer is like obtaining a new asset for your business. Order acquisition describes a complex sale where a team of people is brought in to meet with the prospect's company. This process may include C-level to C-level conversations. It may also involve discussions with marketing, finance, and supply chain experts at both companies. In this scenario, you become an "orchestrator" as much as you remain a salesperson. You have to orchestrate meetings among members of your team and get them working on behalf of members of the buyer's team.

First, however, you must get onto a buyer's radar by seeding, cold-calling, getting a referral, or resorting to some other means of making a connection. You have the initial meeting. You open the conversation about problems and needs. You move to demonstrating your company's capabilities for solving the problem or improving the buyer's business. You present the plan and the pricing and you acquire an order. But that's not where it ends.

You now have an opportunity to go to work for the customer that you put so much effort into selling. The real success is when you get a second or third order from the same customer and obtain referrals to other people in your chief contact's network.

What you believe about selling and closing will drive your behavior. If you believe closing is something you *do* to the buyer, you will act differently than if you believe closing is something the buyer wants as much as you do. What kind of philosophy of selling would you have if you ran a help wanted ad for a sales job with this headline: KILLER WANTED.

I once saw just such an advertisement in the classified section of a prominent trade magazine. The company that placed the ad was looking for a salesperson who was a "killer."

That's an interesting hiring standard.

The ad didn't specify other criteria, like achievement history, written and oral communication skills, integrity, initiative, and empathy.

"Only killers need apply" was the clear message of the ad.

"Why," I wondered, "wasn't the company seeking a professional salesperson with a proven record of sales and customer satisfaction?" And what if that company's customers got wind of the fact that the company only hired "killers" and the "killer" was coming to call on them? No doubt, for the manager who submitted the ad, the word "killer" was meant figuratively.

But the choice of the word indicates that the manager hasn't gotten the message that today's superstars are more like farmers than hunters. They cultivate relationships and don't just "bag" an order. They view their clients as partners instead of prey.

Which is a better philosophy: to see closing as killing or as opening a business relationship that is a win-win for you and the customer?

Closes: Effective and Otherwise

Life is one big sales seminar. I've learned more about selling and closing sales by selling sales training than I've learned in any book or seminar about selling. Here's why. When you sell sales training, the prospects are not only going through your sales process; they are also evaluating how they are being sold and deciding whether they want their salespeople to represent their company the way you are representing yours.

So managers who agree to sit down to talk about buying sales training from me get a free look at what I'm going to teach them. Let me tell you about the day I quit using any closing technique learned from a book, tape, or seminar.

ACCIDENTAL SALES TRAINING SEMINAR

The Stale Close

Early in my career, I was trying to sell a seminar to Charlie Ferguson. He was a general manager who had used other sales trainers and had newly heard of me.

"Chris, I'm interested in bringing you to town. I just have to have the corporate office sign off on it," my prospect said.

That sounded like a buying signal to me. I immediately went for a "trial close" that I had read about and (alas) was teaching in my seminar.

"Well, Charlie," I said (too) smoothly. "If your corporate office approves it, will we be having the seminar in April or would May work better for you?"

"That was a subordinate question, alternate choice close, Chris," said the prospect.

"Yes, it was."

"Well, it didn't work. Good-bye."

Charlie was offended that I would use a technique on him. He wanted a relationship and not just a seminar, and I used a manipulative, old-school closing line.

It took eleven years to gain that trust back and finally do business with Charlie Ferguson.

Accidental Salesperson Axiom:
You don't have to trick people
into doing business with you.

Corollary:
Never use a closing *line* from
any book,tape, or seminar.

Professional buyers go to seminars and learn about the "techniques" that salespeople use to manipulate them. So, the minute you start using those techniques, you lose their trust.

There are, however, some "zero pressure" and "zero manipulation" closes I have come across that I would like to share with you. Yes, you are reading them in a book, but because they are fresh approaches and nonexploitative, it's okay to use them.

1. *"I'd like to have you as a customer. May we get started?"* This approach comes from copywriter Bob Bly's e-book *Zero Pressure Selling*. You could also say, "I'd like to have you as a customer. Is there anything standing in the way of that?" In fact, after reading Bly's book, I e-mailed a training customer who had quit buying during the Great Recession of 2008. "Jeff," I said, "I would love to have you as a customer again. What would have to happen at your end to make that happen?" Within minutes he had e-mailed me back and we put the relationship back together a month later.

2. *"Where do we go from here?"* This line puts the ball in the prospect's court so that you get a clearer picture of what the person's buying process is going to be. It's related to the next example . . .

3. *"What would you like me to do next?"* Notice that by asking the prospect's opinion, you really get a sense of how close or far away you are. Once, while discussing a small purchase of preemployment testing with a

prospect, I posed this very question: "John, what would you like me to do next?"

John answered, "Well, I suppose I could tell you I need to think it over and check out a couple of your competitors. But I am interviewing three people this week and I need these tests now. So why don't you write it up."

"I have no objection to doing that," I said.

4. *"Once you bless this idea, what happens?"* This is the question to ask when you are meeting with an information seeker who is representing a larger buying committee. You are trying to understand the process the company will go through to make a final decision. It is a question that tells you how close or far away the sale is. It can keep you from putting deals with a long buying cycle into your projections too soon.

Closing or Losing?

Closing is a funny word: C - L - O - S - I - N - G. Cross out the C and you are left with another word: L - O - S - I - N - G.

Eighty-six percent of "closing" is "losing."

Accidental sales managers set up this win-lose scenario by emphasizing closing the sale instead of advancing prospects throughout the process.

"Who are you going to close?" This question is asked far more often of salespeople than "Where are you in the process, and what is your strategy for the next step?" Accidental salespeople get beat up in the field and then take more abuse from their managers when they get back to the office. Instead of coaching their people through the process, sales managers add more pressure.

"You didn't close anyone today?"

They run Level 1 sales meetings that focus on the products to sell instead of the prospects' problems and wonder why their salespeople can't seem to close.

I have told my seminar audiences for years about a *Success* magazine survey of a thousand top sales performers. The accompanying article alleged that half of them had abandoned any kind of closing technique. Some 56 percent of the salespeople said they just looked the client in the eye and said something like, "This is right for you. Let's do it." Then they waited for the customer to sign the order.

Belief and Attitude

In order to use this close effectively, you have to believe that what you are offering is right for the prospect, and you have to communicate the *feeling*, not just the closing words.

Let's look at how values, attitudes, and behavior at the time of the sale come together. You ask for the business. Depending on how you ask, you get a *yes*, a *no*, or a *maybe*.

The core of the closing sphere is values. Like most people, you have certain core values that were formed and set in place by the time you were eight. You either looked other people in the eye, told the truth, honored your parents, loved God, and/or shared your toys, or you didn't. Your early childhood experience shaped your values. Your parents and grandparents, older siblings, early religious training, and very first teachers played the biggest roles in forming your values. Let's assume your values are solid. After all, you aren't selling drugs or smuggling arms.

You've heard of wearing your heart on your sleeve? Well, your attitudes and beliefs are more malleable and more visible than your values. You can wake up in the morning ready to take on the marketplace. By nine o'clock you may have a canceled order or get a call from an unhappy customer. By noon, you are reading the want ads.

Here's why belief and attitude are so important in selling. Imagine that you have just made your presentation. The prospect is nodding his head and making positive comments. The prospect's questions indicate a strong interest in what you are selling. Your senses tell you that now is the time to ask for the order.

All of us have "voices" in our head. If you've ever talked to yourself and answered back, then you know there are at least two people in there. But you hear other voices, some of them louder than others.

The voice of the sales trainer says to you, "Look the man in the eye and say, 'This is right for you, let's do it.'"

The voice of the angry customer from this morning shouts in your other ear, "Your quality isn't what it needs to be."

Your mother pipes up and says, "Now don't you lie to the nice man across the desk from you."

You blink twice, your eyes avoid the prospect's eyes, and you mumble, "Well, what do you think?"

The prospect replies, "You made some very interesting points. I'm not sure it's quite right for us. Let me think about it and run it by a few of my people. I'll get back to you."

And just like that you have managed to transmit the doubt created by the unhappy customer from the morning to the prospect you are trying to close in the afternoon. It should be no surprise when you get a *maybe* or a *no*.

People of high integrity have trouble using techniques to sell products they don't believe in. You should maintain your high integrity and work on your belief in your product or service and your company. Otherwise, you will have trouble succeeding in your current sales job.

No Taking "Maybe" for an Answer

Perhaps you've run across the concept that whatever you believe to be true is true, even if it isn't a fact. If you believe that you are a loser if you don't close, you will have a tendency to accept *maybe* for an answer. What if you believed an answer of *maybe* was worse than a *no*? You would act differently.

You know what I mean by a *maybe*:

"That was a great presentation, but see me in ninety days."

"We'll keep you in mind."

"I want to think it over."

Accidental salespeople gladly accept these *maybe*s and put a positive spin on them back at the office. "She's still very interested and I'm going back in ninety days."

If sales managers would yell and scream about *maybe*s, their salespeople would get more decisions and more of those decisions would come in the form of a *yes*.

You've taken the prospect through all sixteen steps in the process and have done a lot of work without getting paid for it. You have sold the prospect on your process. The prospect knows you are making a proposal now and it's time to make a decision.

Producers of infomercials pay for the privilege of making their presentation. They never fail to ask enthusiastically for the order. You too have paid for the privilege of asking for the order with all the work and time you invested. If you have come this far and don't ask, you should feel very bad.

If you ask and don't get the order and get a *maybe*, you should feel horrible. If you ask and get a *no*, you should be glad that you got a decision and focus on the fact that you have nine other active prospects on your Ten Most Wanted List in process. If you get a *yes*, you should feel great and use that momentum.

At this step, a stall or "continuation" is unacceptable. You need to get a decision. If you can't get a decision, you deserve information about why you can't get it. And if you can't get that, you can fall back to getting a date when the decision will be made.

You might say to the prospect, "I would rather have you tell me *no* right now than *maybe*." Then review the steps you've taken and the benefits of the plan. The prospect has time invested in this sale, too. Putting off a decision wastes both your time and hers. You've done a lot of work to earn the business. Use what you've done to make the sale.

Try saying, "May I make a suggestion? If you are trying to let me down easy, I'd prefer to terminate this process now. I'd suggest at the very minimum our next step would be to present this proposal to the full committee, with your endorsement and with me present. Is that feasible?"

Always ask the prospect to take the next step in your process with you. (You have been asking all the way through the process.) The fact that you ask for the order should not come as a great surprise, nor should it come out of the blue.

I've heard all the tricky, manipulative closes. So have your customers. The *no* that means *yes* close has been around for so long, I forgot who I stole it from. The rationale behind it is that it is easier for people to say *no* than *yes*.

When you ask for the order, you want the order, or you want specific information that will help you adjust your proposal so that you can get the order. "Is there any reason why we can't go ahead with this proposal?" is a question that will elicit either a *no*—which means the prospect is now a customer—or a *yes*, in which case you should get a specific objection that you can handle. After you deal with the objection, ask again: "Now, is there any reason we can't do business?"

"No."

"Thank you. Please sign here."

Seven Strategies for Preventing Objections

In the next two sections of this chapter, we are going to deal with preventing objections and handling objections. Objections occur not just at the end of your presentation, but throughout the selling process. Prospects object to meeting with you, to revealing vital information about their problems, to your price, and even to taking action.

Preventing objections may be a more important skill than handling objections. Dale Carnegie said it this way: "The best way to win an argument is to avoid it."

The late famed golf pro Harvey Penick once told the story about a student who came to him for a lesson to help him get out of sand traps. Penick recommended that he first take a lesson on how to keep the ball on the fairway.

Prevent as many objections as you can. Handling objections is a must-have selling skill. "Resistance is the reason for the existence of salespeople," the saying goes. At the same time, you shouldn't have to fight your way to every sale. Here are seven strategies to help you thwart objections before you are forced to handle them.

1. *Work on your beliefs about selling and rejection by putting your systems (not yourself) on the line.* If you believe that you are putting yourself on the line every day in selling, then rejection may hurt you more than it should.

   Here's a slightly different way to think about selling. Don't put yourself on the line; put your proposal on the line (or rather, on the table). There's a big difference.

   Sure, you've got to have a strong ego drive to make sales. You've got to want to succeed. But you don't have to take every *no* as a personal affront. They are saying *no* to your proposal, not to you.

   Earlier in this book I described a seven-step appointment-getting system. I recommended sending prospects an article about an issue or trend in their industry, along with a business card. The first contact is simply a business card attached to an article with a brief note ("Thought you might be interested in this") written right on the business card. The next step is to send another article, and then a couple of days later to send the letter.

   You've discovered that sending a couple of articles, the letter, and following up with a telephone call dramatically increases the number of calls taken and appointments booked. Using a system like this prevents some rejection.

   If after sending a couple of articles and the letter, the prospect still doesn't want to meet with you, the prospect hasn't rejected you; he's rejected your appointment-getting system. You haven't put yourself on the line; you've put your appointment-getting system on the line. You don't have to say *you* got rejected. You can say instead that this system worked 40 percent of the time. You can either accept a 40 percent closing ratio or work to improve the system.

You aren't putting *yourself* on the line. You are putting your systems on the line. And you can always improve your systems.

Of course, the only way you can blame your system is to have one. Systematizing your approach to selling is part of building your money machine. Learning to realistically label what happens to you is a powerful rejection-prevention strategy.

Instead of saying, "I blew that proposal," say, "He rejected my proposal, not me. I worked for three hours putting it together. I learned what he doesn't like and I can present it to him again, in three weeks."

2. *Control what you ask for, especially early in the process. Don't try to go too far, too fast.* On the first phone call or the first cold contact, you are selling the prospect on meeting with you, not on buying your product or service.

One script that has worked well for many salespeople is this: "I don't know if you should be using my product or not. That's why the first meeting we have is a non-decision-making, fact-finding call."

The purpose of this script is to reduce any tension or apprehension your prospect may have and to advance the process to the next level. It's much better than muttering the trite, "Your account has just been assigned to me, and I want to learn a little about your business so that I can help you." There's a big difference in the way you'll be perceived and received.

3. *Do not ask for an appointment with the new prospect this afternoon or tomorrow morning.* Remember to ask the prospect for the appointment next week. It's much easier to schedule you into a blank calendar than into an already-crazy schedule. If you ask for the appointment next week, you won't seem desperate for the meeting. If you *are* desperate for the meeting, it is even more important that you appear not to be desperate for the meeting.

Remember: Think of selling as a series of advances—little closes that lead to the order. Before every call, think about how you are going to advance the sale. Also think about your fallback position if the prospect says *no* to your first suggestion.

4. *Use the magic phrase, "This is the way I work."* Tell the prospect how you work and what is going to happen so that she doesn't have to defend against your sales tactics.

   Get the prospect to buy the way you sell first, before you try to sell your product or service. For one thing, selling the prospect on the way you sell is an easier sale to close. And for another, it sets up the rest of the call. Use the phrase, "This is the way I work," and then lay out the steps in your sales process and the work you propose to do to earn the prospect's business.

5. *Get in the last word.* Sales is a series of defeats, punctuated by profitable victories. You are not going to win them all. But when you lose, you have the right to politely voice your opinion. For example, you can say:

   I worked very hard on this presentation in order to earn your business, and I'm sorry you didn't decide to go with this plan. But I do appreciate the fact that you told me *no* instead of *maybe*. I once read that great salespeople take rejection as information instead of taking it personally. What could I have done differently on this proposal?

   Or you might say something like this:

   John, I've made three presentations to you, and we've had twelve meetings together, and you have yet to purchase anything from me. I'm going to give you a three-month hiatus. I'm not giving up. I'm just going to retool my approach and see if we can come at it in a different way. Fair enough? In the meantime, I'm going to need some other people to meet with. May I ask you for a referral of a businessperson I might be able to help?

This is a form of giving up without giving up. When you offer to go on hiatus, the prospect may tell you what's really keeping you two from doing business. At the very worst, you'll get some decent referrals. You've taken control of a situation that wasn't going anywhere anyway.

6. *Work by referrals.* Always ask your prospects if you can use their names as a reference. Ask them if they know someone they feel you could help. Ask them about a specific prospect on your list that you are having trouble with. Ask them, occasionally, if they would make a call or send a letter on your behalf.

7. *Drop names of successful clients you work with when talking to a new prospect.* Don't overdo it, but understand that prospects want to know you have helped others. If you are brand-new to the industry, discuss your other sales experiences and your education and how that has prepared you to help the prospect.

   The point is, you should be sharing information instead of pitching product. Share information with prospects about business issues; trends in their own industry; and, yes, even your own background.

   You are not a machine. You have feelings that can be hurt and beliefs that can be shaken. But you are building a money machine and systematizing much of your selling process. You are not putting yourself on the line. You are putting your systems on the line. And you can always improve your systems.

Nine Strategies for Handling Objections

You prevent objections by preparing for your call, by qualifying prospects better, and by demonstrating that you understand the prospect's business and needs before presenting your solution.

Going through your selling process and telling the client what is going to happen heads off a lot of objections. Still, some prospects will object to meeting with you. Other prospects will object to your price. And yet other prospects will object because they don't see any need for your product. Here are nine strategies for handling the objections that you can't (or didn't) prevent.

1. *Don't answer the first objection.* Most first objections aren't substantial enough even to deal with. Prospects give you their standard objection that gets rid of most salespeople: "I want to think it over." "Your price is too high." "We had a bad experience with your company." "I don't have enough time to meet with you." You can't "handle" these objections until you quantify or qualify them. Therefore, you need to be very conscious of strategy 2.

2. *Reverse all objections.* Reversing simply means giving the objection back to the prospect for that person to expand upon. The prospect says, "Your price is too high." You say, "When you say our price is too high, that means . . .?" Reversing is a powerful strategy espoused by the late sales trainer David Sandler. Reversing should get you enough information so that you can deal with a true objection. Example: "Your competitor is only charging $172,000, and you're asking $195,000." Now you know you are $23,000 apart, and you can sell the prospect on why your proposal is worth $23,000 more.

3. *Count to three before answering any objection.* Listen carefully, and consider what the prospect is saying before you jump in with your side of the story. As you may have guessed, your silence might also act as a kind of reverse. If you don't answer the objection right away, the prospect may feel compelled to add critical information.

4. *Agree with the objection and use the energy behind it.* Agreeing with the objection is one of the most underutilized but

most powerful strategies available to you. Finding some-thing you and the prospect can agree on actually builds rapport. Tapping into the prospect's feelings and not just the prospect's words helps you determine just how important the objection is. Here's an example:

"Your price is ridiculous!" the prospect says, to which you reply, "We have the highest-priced widget on the market today. You're absolutely right. You sound angry about that." Then you listen.

Oftentimes the prospect will say something like, "I'm not angry. You have a right to charge whatever you want to charge." You can then come back with a question: "Are you willing to look at how we can ultimately save you money, or is price the only criteria?" Then you are creating an opportunity to go into all the things your product does that your competitors' products don't.

5. *Agree with the feeling, if not the content.* Sometimes the prospect gives you an objection that's so ill-founded you can't agree with it. At that point, you might have to agree with the prospect's feeling instead of the content of the objection.

"Your quality is subpar," the prospect says. In this case, you can reply: "I understand how you may feel that way. And at the same time, in the past five years we've completely transformed our engineering department, and the new vice president of engineering has gradually raised the standards, so I can confidently say we now can exceed your expectations in that regard."

Often you are called on to defend the company's honor and make strong statements to refute prospect misinformation or competitors' disinformation. Agreeing with the feeling and acknowledging the prospect's right to have it helps set up your strong rebuttal while softening the delivery, which makes it less confrontational.

6. *Tell a story.* At this stage of your career you've no doubt heard of the feel-felt-found method of handling objections: "You know, Mr. Jones, I know how you *feel*. Ed Whitlock over at Acme Widgets *felt* the same way. But when Acme's people implemented our system, they *found* huge cost-reduction benefits and increased reliability."

   This is a very formulaic approach. Your job is to tell a story about a client who is benefiting from the same product or service your prospect objects to, and to package that story in such a way that it reaches the prospect emotionally and logically and eliminates the objection.

   Story-based selling is a powerful tool that bypasses arguments by conjuring up a third party to whom all the benefits have already accrued. The prospect can't argue with the success of one of your happy clients. That's why stories are so powerful.

7. *Express curiosity or interest.* Sometimes an objection is so off-the-wall that it surprises you, because you've never heard it before. In that case, honesty is the best policy.

   You can say, for instance, "Really? You are the first person who's ever complained about slow delivery times. I'm curious. Where did that idea come from?"

   As you can see, this is a type of reversing strategy, but your incredulity should be honest and not feigned. Truth is better than creativity.

8. *Confront with the brutal truth.* When the prospect says, "See me in ninety days," you should reply directly and with a question: "John, it's been my experience that as soon as I walk out the door, you will quit thinking about my proposal. Usually 'see me in ninety days' means there's a part of my proposal I haven't handled well. What is your main concern with what I've presented, and what has to change in ninety days for us to do business?"

9. *Give the panic button answer.* Finally, it's a good idea to memorize the panic button answer to any objection a prospect could think of. The panic button answer is, "I understand"—pause—"and at the same time . . ."

   Here's an example:

   OBJECTION: I had a bad experience with your company.

   ANSWER: I understand. And at the same time, time passes and things do change. I mean, I'm new, the district manager's new, and we've made some major improvements in our product line. What will it take to make things right with you and move on?

Prospects often object because they want to test your convictions and see what you're made of, not just to blow you off. They challenge you to learn your business and earn their business. You need to rise to that challenge.

An objection is a wonderful thing, because if there were no objections, the *first* salesperson to make the call would make the sale instead of the *best* person making the sale.

As a buyer, I wanted someone to engage me and challenge me to do something different. Your prospects want the same thing from you.

When you control the focus, you control the meeting. What is the prospect's problem that your company, your creativity, your being on the account and adding value can solve? When you focus on helping the prospect get what he wants instead of what you want to sell him, you get fewer objections and make more sales.

Two Powerful Thoughts

Let me leave you with two powerful thoughts that may change your whole philosophy of selling.

1. You don't have to prove someone wrong for you to be right.

2.   That's true because two points of view *can* exist simultaneously.

These two thoughts can make selling less stressful for you and your prospects. Instead of a debate you find *common ground*.

The secret to building rapport with a prospect is to find something you both agree on and build from there, instead of debating insignificant things.

Life is not a contest.

The best way to handle objections is to prevent them. Thorough preparation, professional questioning, and careful listening are required. If you answer all your prospect's questions as they arise, your prospect will have no objections to raise. When objections arise, you've got some strategies for handling them. The main strategy is always to get more information before you try to handle an objection.

One of the most important lessons in this book is: You don't have to prove someone wrong in order for you to be right. Two points of view can exist simultaneously. Put aside the need for one-upmanship. Concentrate instead on finding common ground.

PART FOUR

Managing Your Career

CHAPTER 13

Setting New Standards, Surpassing Old Limits

You rarely think about all the standards your parents set for you. But chances are the last time you went to an all-you-can-eat buffet, you started at the salad bar instead of the dessert table.

If your parents set standards and defined limits when you were growing up, consider yourself very fortunate indeed. These standards become habits that keep you healthy, safe, and even make you prosperous.

No Dessert Until You Finish Your Peas

These are a few of the standards I grew up with:

- One-half hour of television per night—*after* you've finished your homework.
- In bed with the lights out at nine o'clock sharp on school nights.
- No dessert until you finish you peas.
- Save 10 percent of your lawn-mowing money.

Parents inevitably put up with a lot of whining as their children test their resolve and try to extend the limits.

"You're too strict."

"But, Mom, everybody's parents let them stay out until midnight."

"I didn't ask to be born."

Great parents set standards and hold their children accountable. When their kids grow up they have more self-discipline. They can "self-manage."

Self-management is critical to your sales success.

One of the great things about selling is the tremendous amount of freedom it affords. Your boss isn't constantly looking over your shoulder. One of the *worst* things about selling is the tremendous amount of freedom it affords you. Take your choice.

For undisciplined salespeople with lax standards, this freedom is a recipe for disaster. They can drive around aimlessly passing prospect after prospect. Sometimes you can find them purposefully driving golf balls at the range. (Just because you have a smartphone doesn't mean you're working.)

Children learn just how much they can get away with before parents intervene. Discipline can be as mild as a stern look or a time-out. Discipline can escalate to loss of privileges and being "grounded." Parents discipline you so that, ultimately, you behave in a disciplined way all by yourself.

Your company probably sets certain performance standards for you. A standard is a measurable indicator of performance, often involving a consequence. If your work doesn't conform to certain standards, there may be extra meetings for you, coaching, pleading, probation, and finally termination.

Many salespeople try to test the limits their managers will tolerate. They turn in their call reports a couple of days late, knock off early on Friday afternoons, and save much of their creativity for their sales reports.

At the same time, many companies have wishes instead of standards. When sales managers complain to me about the lack of effort on behalf of their salespeople, it often sounds like this:

"I wish my salespeople were more proactive and less reactive."

"I wish my people would get to work on time."

"I wish they would write better proposals."

"I wish my salespeople would make more calls."

Let's define self-management as performing enough steps in your selling process every day, week, and month at a high enough quality in order to deny yourself the unpleasant opportunity of failing or getting fired. Setting higher standards than your company sets for you is one way to surpass old limits you placed on yourself.

Accidental Salesperson Axiom:
Your objective isn't to set high standards
for yourself and your sales career.

Corollary:
You set high standards so that you
can achieve your objectives.

An objective or goal is what you want to happen at a certain time. "On May 31, two years from now, I will have booked an additional $3,000,000 in new business."

Many sales books and far too many motivational speakers will tell you the importance of setting goals. Yet many unsuccessful salespeople have very high goals. Setting goals alone isn't the answer. So what's the missing ingredient?

Setting higher *performance standards* is the key to helping you achieve your higher goals.

Think of it this way. The goal is the "what." The standards are the "how."

Let's look at how standards and objectives work together. I'll start with a story.

The Miracle in Pikeville, Kentucky

There are breaks at my seminars, but I rarely get to take one. Someone always wants to talk about something. At a seminar at Barren

River State Park Lodge near Glasgow, Kentucky, one of the participants approached me during the morning break. I recognized Connie from the year before. She shook my hand and then put her left
hand on my right hand and held it there for a long time. She looked
into my eyes and said, "Chris"—it sounded like *Chree-us*—"after
your seminar last year I increased my sales by $7,000! Thank you."

She actually sounded excited about a number that didn't do
much for me.

"That's nice, Connie," I said without much enthusiasm.

"Seven thousand dollars a month," she added.

I squeezed her hand a little harder, shook it enthusiastically,
and said, "That's very good. Congratulations!"

She just smiled and said, "In Pikeville, Kentucky, that's a miracle."

It does sometimes seem miraculous how much more money
your prospects can come up with when you align your behavior
with the things they value. However, these kinds of stories happen
so often to our students that we no longer label them miraculous.

Connie had simply changed the way she did things as a result
of the previous year's seminar. She set some new standards and
surpassed her old limits.

Your Personal Seven-Minute, Do-It-Yourself Sales Stimulus Program

Here is a simple exercise you can do to see exactly how objectives
and standards work together. It requires seven minutes of silence on
your part and a little bit of thinking and note taking. These will be
the most profitable seven minutes you can spend today, so do it now.

Pick a number that represents a significant increase in your
sales. Connie thought $7,000 a month was a miracle. Pick your
own number and your own time frame. You may want to consider
an entire quarter or even a full year. This is your objective (goal).

Enter the number on the worksheet provided here, or on a
blank sheet of paper. (I've included a PDF of this form at
www.TheAccidentalSalesperson2012.com). Then make a list of

twenty things that would have to happen for you to increase your sales by that number and in the time frame you've indicated. By listing twenty ideas instead of two or three, you are telling your brain to go to work for you and to think beyond the obvious and easy answers. Please do this sales-boosting exercise right now and we'll work with your list once you have it completed.

* * *

What would have to happen for me to increase my sales by _____ per _____?

1. _____

2. _____

3. _____

4. _____

5. _____

6. _____

7. _____

8. _____

9. _____

10. _____

11. _____

12. _____

13. _____

14. _____

15. _____

16. _____

17. _____

18. _____

19. _____

20. _____

* * *

You have just started the process of setting higher standards for yourself.

To achieve the bigger dollar figure, you have to set higher standards. You have both your new objective—the increased dollar figure you want to sell—and you have a list of things that need to happen in order for you to achieve it. I predict that most of them involve your taking specific actions that lead to sales. Many of the things on your list involve higher standards of performance than you are accomplishing now. You know you have to hold yourself to these higher standards in order to accomplish the stretch goal you put down.

Thousands of people have completed this exercise in my seminars. The first question I ask after giving everyone seven minutes of silence is, "What was that exercise like for you?" There have been a variety of answers.

One participant said, "I now see exactly what I need to do to get better. If you had told me I needed to do these things, I would have resisted. But when I wrote them down, they meant more to me."

People rarely resist their own ideas.

"I now realize that I have more control over my sales than I thought I did," said another salesperson.

"I'm mad," said a third one. "If I had been doing the things I already know I need to do, I would have been making higher commissions all along."

So you now have an objective and a list of twenty ideas to help you achieve that objective. You're off to a good start, but the chances are good that your standards aren't quite up to my standards for *writing* standards just yet.

Let's work with the list you created to make sure you have measurable indicators of performance. Let me guess at a few of the things you wrote down. A typical list looks like this the first time through:

- Get better organized.

- Do more prospecting.

- Ask for more referrals.

- Write better proposals.

- Ask for bigger orders.

Very noble ideas, but hardly measurable, and a standard has to be measurable. If your list looks like this and if you stop there, you will be like most accidental salespeople who have a vague idea that they should be doing more than they are and doing it better. They just never define what "more" means and what "better" looks like. They have frail wishes instead of solid standards.

"No dessert until you finish your peas" is a standard.

"Get better organized" will be a wish unless and until you can describe what becoming better organized means, from a behavioral standpoint. Having a standard for being organized will also let you know exactly how to get back on track when you are disorganized. If you want to "get better organized" and have it be a measurable indicator of performance, you need to rewrite this item on your list.

Most of us are familiar with quantity standards. There are also quality standards, timeliness standards, and cost standards.

Quantity standards are those you can measure by counting. For example, "I will send out two prospecting letters every week."

Quality standards are somewhat more objective, but still measurable. For instance, "I will have Jane proofread my letters and proposals so there are no typos." Or "I will include at least two Level 2 pages and one Level 3 page in my written proposals."

Timeliness standards can be measured by a watch or calendar. "I will return e-mails within ninety minutes," or "I will call every active customer every ten business days to offer an upgrade or an idea."

Cost standards are measured by dollars. There might be a standard for reimbursing you for business lunches at a maximum of $40. Or there might be a standard for spending $X to entertain your ten best clients during the course of the year.

Now, what would "getting better organized" look like if you actually got better organized? Here are some possibilities:

- Take fifteen minutes to plan and prioritize my to-do list. (Timeliness standard)

- Keep one project on my desk at a time. (Quantity standard)

- Schedule a one-hour appointment with myself daily to work on a profitable project. (Quality and Timeliness standards)

- Research and invest up to $149 in new sales-tracking software, or find an app for my smartphone. Have it up and running in two weeks. (Cost and Quality standard)

At the end of the day, you can measure whether you worked to those standards or not. If you did, you are better organized and you know why. If you only took ten minutes to plan, there is a gap between the standard you set for yourself and your actual performance. If there are piles of paper on your desk instead of one project, you are not working to the standard.

The concept of "closing the gap" between the standard and your actual performance is what gives standards their power. Think of it this way. If your actual performance falls short of the standard, you have a gap. Your standard is fifteen minutes of planning, and for three days (Monday through Wednesday), your actual performance has fallen short (see Figure 13-1). You have a gap. By closing the gap, you will get your performance back on track, or back to the standard you set for yourself.

Self-managers understand the power of managing the gap and not the goal. They set higher goals and hold themselves to higher standards. Set the goal, and then set the standards that will help you reach your goal. Let's convert one other wish into a measurable standard of performance.

Figure 13-1 Gap management is something you can do so your sales manager doesn't have to.

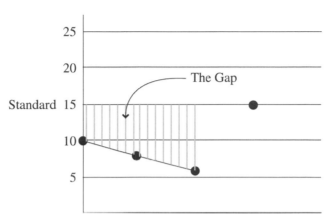

"Do more prospecting" is a wish. "Send out ten seeds per week" is a standard. You can check it off when you do it. You can graph it. You know when you don't do it. You feel terribly guilty about it and close the gap.

Accidental salespeople don't understand how much control they have in sales and therefore don't take control of their careers. When you are selling on purpose you start to focus on performance and not just sales. If you follow sports and read about your favorite team in the newspapers, you've seen box scores. Box scores give you the details of how the final score was put on the board. To true fans, the *how* is far more interesting than the *what* (the final score). Managers use the information from the box scores to plot their strategies for the next game. It's the analysis of the "game within the game" that yields usable information, not the final score.

Great salespeople understand the game within the game. They don't sell by accident. They analyze every move they make carefully. Their standards allow them to achieve their objectives. They are always on the lookout for something they can do to gain control of the sales process.

Accidental salespeople sense they need to be doing more, but are not specific about what "more" means. They want to do "better," but lack the quality standards that let them know when they actually are doing better. The proposal-writing template from Chapter 10 may help you do more with less. Many salespeople have discovered that they can sell more by making five Level 2 presentations than they can by making ten Level 1 presentations. Working to specific standards doesn't necessarily mean working longer and harder.

Look at the list of twenty items you created. Go through it and pick the four or five best ideas for achieving your new objective for increased dollar sales. Now convert those ideas into standards. Make them measurable indicators of your performance by adding a quality, quantity, timeliness, and/or cost component.

Don't go crazy. Pick just one standard of the four or five and implement it for the next twenty-one days. Perhaps you have heard the adage that it takes twenty-one days to establish a habit. Good habits don't require constant monitoring. You just do them. Once you have converted your standard into a new habit, you can set another standard and work on that for twenty-one days.

At this pace, you can create seventeen new habits per year! See how easy it is if you take small steps?

All that is left is to commit yourself to tracking your performance and holding yourself accountable to those standards you implement. Keep track of your performance daily, weekly, and monthly. If you start to fall below the standard, close the gap quickly.

"Shovel the piles when they are small" is the best advice for accidental salespeople who have decided to hold themselves to a higher standard. Don't wait until your actual performance gets so far below your standard that you can't get it back up without extreme effort. For example, let's say you set a standard to write three (quantity) Level 2 (quality) proposals per week, but only manage to write two of them this week. Close the gap next week by writing four proposals. If you only write two proposals two weeks in a row, you'll need to write five proposals the third week. Now you've got a big pile of work to do. Close the gap when it is small.

If you want to achieve your objectives without kissing your home life good-bye, you need to grasp how objectives and standards work together. For too many accidental salespeople, the only answer they can come up with is to work harder and longer in order to sell more. Since they are already working longer and harder than they ever thought they would, they become discouraged.

You are going to do it differently. You are going to increase your sales by doing everything better. You are already seeing that you can get more out of every single prospect interaction by simply choosing to approach your prospects at Level 2 and by having more Level 3 and 4 "moments" and including Level 3 and 4 pages in your proposals.

Holding yourself to higher standards is the final refinement.

To help you get off to a fast start with standard setting, consider adapting the following list of standards. Each standard contains a blank that you fill in so that it is your number and reflects your reality.

Suggested Standards for Accidental Salespeople Who Have Chosen to Sell on Purpose

- Take _____ minutes to plan each day and prioritize my action list.
- Ask _____ customers per _____ for a referral.
- Get into position to ask prospects for $ _____ per _____ .
- Have _____ (quantity) prospects in process and track them on my _____ (quantity) Most Wanted List.
- Make a minimum of _____ new business moves weekly. (Each time you move one prospect one step in your process, it counts as one new business move.)
- Write a minimum of _____Level _____ proposals per _____ .
- Attend _____ sales seminar(s) or personal improvement program(s) per _____ .
- Send _____ articles (seeds) per _____ to prospects.

- Send _____ articles per _____ to current customers.
- Read for _____ minutes/hour(s) per _____ in my field to become an expert.
- Dial the phone a minimum of _____ times per _____.
- Wash my car _____ per _____.
- Shine my shoes _____ per _____.
- Rehearse any presentation for more than $ _____ with my sales manager.
- Arrive _____ minutes before any firm appointment with a prospect or customer.
- Return phone calls within _____ minutes/hour(s) of receiving them.
- Write down everything I promise or tell a prospect or customer I am going to do and act on that promise. (Or use the voice recorder on my smartphone to record my promises and review them daily.)
- Convert a customer needs analysis meeting into a written proposal within _____ business days.
- Book the next meeting or "scheduled sales conversation" or service call within _____ business days.

This certainly is not meant to be an exhaustive list—nor is every standard appropriate for every company or salesperson. It is merely meant to get you past the "make more calls" mentality. Your standards will be better than mine precisely because they are your standards.

Start with the objective and then write your standards. You will immediately gain control by choosing to change your focus. When you quit focusing on sales and start measuring the performance that leads to sales, you are selling on purpose. The disciplined approach to selling will earn you new respect and a lot more money. And there's an added benefit.

Your parents will be so proud of you.

CHAPTER 14

Building Relationships Your Competitors Can't Steal

I'm not sure why the subject came up, but over dinner, my friend Burt started telling me about his credit card. "They charge me $350 a year, Chris, but they give me one percent cash back on every purchase I make. So I buy everything with that credit card. At the end of the year, I come out about $450 ahead."

You want happy customers telling their friends about the great product they bought from you and the wonderful benefits they receive as a result of their loyalty to you.

Making the Sale Is the End of the Sixteen-Step Process, and the Beginning of the Business Relationship

I have never thought of the first sale as the "end" of the process. My goal has always been to create a customer who will be a great source of profitable repeat business and referrals, which are always the warmest leads. The best advice I can give you is to work at least as hard on managing the relationship as you did making the sale.

Customer service is given plenty of lip service today. But you need a measurable standard for service, just like you need standards to achieve your sales objectives. If you were going to provide good service, what would it look like? What does your customer expect? Have you spelled out your service process so that a buyer knows what she's getting after she decides to buy?

In the post 9/11 era, flying is no longer something I look forward to. Even so, the airlines have a great model for customer recognition and extra service—the frequent flyer program. Airlines reward their frequent flyers for flying, not for threatening to fly.

Rewarding Customers for Buying, Not for Threatening to Buy

I completed an around-the-world speaking tour that included stops in Sydney, Australia; Auckland and Rotorua, New Zealand; Berlin, Germany; and Brighton, Oxford, Maidstone, and Manchester, England. Thirty-five days and more than 25,000 miles in the air.

Here's the discovery I made on that trip: I hate flying.

At the same time, I love to be upgraded.

On the ten-and-a-half-hour leg from Bangkok to Frankfurt, the Thai Airways reservationist moved me from business class to first class. I still wear the pajamas they gave me and tell everyone about the full reclining seats and how little jet lag you get when you sleep through the night.

Years before, I was returning from an easy nine-day speaking trip. The flight attendant came up to me and said, "Mr. Little, what would you like for dinner once we are airborne?"

"It's Lytle," I gently corrected her, stressing the long "i" sound.

"Oh, I'm terribly sorry."

"That's okay. It happens all the time."

"But Mr. Lytle, you are a 100K Premier Executive, one of our very best customers, and I want to get your name right."

"Well, thank you."

Now, I know that this flight attendant had never seen me before and would likely never see me again. And I knew that she knew my name because of the printout that the gate agent gave her. And

I knew that the frequent flyer status is on that sheet because of the computer.

But I didn't care.

It's nice to be recognized as an important customer and called by name.

Just before we landed, the flight attendant came back and whispered something in my ear. "Do you like wine, Mr. Lytle?"

"Why, yes I do."

"We have a bottle of Chardonnay left over." She opened the overhead bin. "Is this your suitcase?"

"Yes."

She opened my suitcase and carefully placed the bottle of wine inside. "I just saw how many cities you've been to on this trip and how many United legs you've taken. Thanks for flying United, Mr. Lytle."

"You're welcome, and thank you."

Sarah was waiting for me at baggage claim when I got home.

"Hi, honey. How was your trip?" she asked. I unzipped my suitcase and grasped the neck of the bottle and held it up like it was some kind of trophy. "They gave me a bottle of wine," I said grinning. "United Airlines *noticed* me!"

The airlines define a "frequent flyer" as someone who takes three round-trips a year. You can see why they try to build loyalty with frequent flyers like me. If United loses me, they need about twenty frequent flyers to make up for my volume and mileage.

They know it. *You* need to know what losing a big customer means to you. How many average customers will it take to make up the difference? Then you can act intelligently and accordingly to build a major customer follow-up program.

Accidental Salesperson Axiom:
Even customers who don't love to buy from you love
to be recognized as an important customer.

Corollary:
Every customer is silently (or not so silently)
crying, "Notice me!"

To this day, United Airlines gets around 70 percent of my business.

Think of this airline analogy when prospects ask you for discounts and deals. I have looked prospects in the eye and said, "I will reward you when you become a good customer, but right now you are only threatening to buy. Once you become a top-tier customer, here's what you can expect . . ."

Then I show the prospect our customer rewards program.

If you decided to have a "frequent buyer program," use it as a selling tool like the airlines do. People like perks.

The Platinum Service Checklist

The Platinum Service Checklist (Figure 14-1) is the tool that helps you implement a service program. It may be the most important tool in this book. Repeat business is more profitable than new business. You are now selling on purpose and closing more sales. Not losing customers you already have is the final piece of the puzzle.

If you cannot benefit from repeat business, read no further. If, however, your business relies on selling more to the same clients or on forging strong relationships throughout their companies, this is for you. You can download additional copies of the Platinum Service Checklist at www.TheAccidentalSalesperson2012.com.

This checklist offers nineteen suggested customer "touches" you could perform over the course of a year. Some of these touches, such as writing a thank-you note or sending a St. Patrick's Day card with a Pot of Gold lottery ticket in it, can be performed in five minutes. Other touches involve more highly orchestrated activities, like inviting customers to your facility or arranging a visit from top management to their facility. You can take a customer to lunch or invite a customer to your company's skybox for a college or pro game. If you don't have a skybox, you can share a ticket to a sporting event.

If a customer's spend is in your top 5 percent or 10 percent of all customers, you might add perks. If the customer is a smaller

Figure 14-1 Platinum service plan.

	Jan	Feb	Mar	Apr	May	Jun	Jul	Aug	Sep	Oct	Nov	Dec
Write and send thank-you note												
Place follow-up phone call #1												
Send article with business card												
Invite for tour of your facility												
Have a social interaction												
Have top management send letter												
Attend sporting event												
Follow-up phone call #2												
Set results evaluation meeting												
Entertain client												
Provide helpful phone numbers												
Send birthday card												
Send holiday card												
Clip article about client interest												
Donate to client cause												
Send relevant business book												
Send specialty item												
Invite to seminar/webinar												
Invite to a golf outing												

Enter the projected date of the event. Circle the date when you've accomplished your Platinum Service touch.

one, you might decide to do a few of the suggested "touches" instead of all nineteen. You can also piggyback on my suggestions
and come up with nineteen more of your own ideas.

Look at a one-year tracking program for your customer. Count
how many touches you actually provide. How much recognition do
you give your top clients? A trip to The Masters is unforgettable. If
your response is "Forget about that," then a series of personalized
touches can help to solidify the relationship.

If you have a service department, you may be doing these
things already. The big idea is to put customers into a service
process, just like you put prospects into your sales process. They
are still hearing from your competitors. They really need to hear
from you so that they feel important.

Repeat business is profitable business. You already have the relationship, so the selling cycle is shorter. As you might expect, the
best training I ever received on how to do great customer service
happened quite by accident.

ACCIDENTAL SERVICE TRAINING SEMINAR

The Cruise

Sarah and I were on our first Royal Caribbean cruise. We were very excited
about it. I read the cruise brochure our travel agent gave us three times.
It advertised a fun-filled week.

And the pictures! The brochure had pictures of beautiful people—
men and women—in stunning bathing suits, sunning themselves around
a crystal clear pool. In the pictures were smooth seas, sunny days, sump-
tuous midnight buffets, and luxurious ports of call. The brochure sold the
experience and helped us visualize and anticipate what was in store for
us when we stepped aboard the *Sun Viking*.

Except the reality didn't exactly match the brochure.

I was expecting a cruise like the ones I had seen in the brochure. It
was the same ship, all right. And there were the same bathing suits, but
they weren't on the same models that were in the brochure. (There are
certain people—men and women—who shouldn't wear bikinis.)

And there were children in the swimming pool. And you know what children do in swimming pools. No brochure writer would mention it, but I will.

I'll tell you something else. Nobody ever gets seasick reading a brochure. But once you are on the open ocean, it's a different story. The motion of a ship at sea is not something you can practice getting used to. Either you can handle it or you can't.

In the brochure the people are suntanned. In reality, the people on the deck chairs, including Sarah and I, were wedding-dress white, Wisconsin people.

There is nothing like a mai tai in the morning. I mean, in the brochure, people drink them, right? Wrong. In the brochure, they are props for the models in the beautiful bathing suits.

Now, two hours into the cruise, an interesting thing happens. You mix a couple of early-in-the-day drinks with four hours in the subtropical sun and the undulating motion of the ship and you realize on the first day of the cruise—this isn't what I was expecting!

It's hard to eat a scrumptious dinner while in a seasick-hung-over-sunburned state. You can't eat all you can eat when you feel as bad as you've ever felt.

Six days to go.

On the second day it was cloudy. They don't show clouds in cruise brochures. But that was okay. We didn't need any more sun.

Things got better eventually, and we enjoyed our new friends and some of the ports we visited. Still, I remember thinking how I probably wouldn't take another cruise any time soon. On the next to the last day, the cruise director organized a meeting of all first-time cruisers.

"It's time to evaluate your first Royal Caribbean cruise," announced the cruise director. "Our staff members are passing out the evaluation forms for you. But before you fill them out, I'd like to go through each part of the evaluation with you."

The cruise director on the *Sun Viking* had a very important job: to manage the experience of the cruisers—first-time cruisers especially.

He did one of the best post-selling jobs at the end of the cruise I have ever seen.

"Now, the first thing we're going to rate is the entertainment," he said. "Before you make your evaluation, I want to review the week with you. Did all of you see the comedian at the late-night show?"

About half the room clapped and I turned to Sarah and smiled, remembering how funny he had been.

"And every night we have had a Las Vegas–style show," he said. "Remember the magician? How about the Broadway-style dance review?"

More applause.

"When we stop at a port, these entertainers get off and meet or are flown to other ships. That way you get a new show every night. It means that whatever Royal Caribbean cruise you take, you'll get great entertainment. Now, folks," the cruise director said, "please rate us on the entertainment."

Sarah and I circled the highest rating.

"Another thing we want you to rate is the bar service. On Royal Caribbean, we do not push drinks, but we want them to be available when you want them. Our standard is ninety-second service. And to do this, we have a lot of servers and a host of bartenders. The drinks aren't free, because not everyone wants to drink, so that keeps the cruise price down. But our goal is to charge what you'd pay in a local tavern and not an expensive hotel. Before you rate our bar service," he said, "I'd like to ask our entire bartending and serving crew to come in. Please give them a round of applause."

Wild, enthusiastic applause.

"Now I'd like you to rate our cabin steward service. Our goal is to service your cabin and never disturb you. So we'll never knock on your door and disturb you to clean your cabin. But we know when you're not in there. How do we know? It's a Royal Caribbean secret. But we know. So whenever you leave, our cabin steward is in there tidying up. That's why you always have clean towels. That's why your shoes are always stowed under your bed and your bed is always made. When you come back, everything is neat and tidy. Shipshape. Ladies and gentleman, the Royal Caribbean cabin crew," he said, while ushering the crew to step forward. "Please give them a hand and write down your rating."

You have probably guessed by now that despite my early impressions, I gave Royal Caribbean excellent ratings and have returned for another cruise. But I doubt that I would have, had our cruise director not shown the work that had been done behind the scenes.

People don't know what you're doing for them unless you tell them. Find a way to share the behind-the-scenes information.

Cruise companies can't control the weather or the seas, so they control as much of the experience as they can and tell you exactly what they are doing to make your experience the best it can possibly be.

What about you? You're not just a salesperson; you're a cruise director. You are managing the expectations of your clients and not just making sales. If you want something that you do to be more valuable, you need to tell your clients what you are doing.

Selling is teaching. Teaching is selling.

Teach your clients what you do for them that no one else is doing and good things happen. You get customers who are more loyal to you and customers who are willing to pay more for what you're selling, because they now know all the work that goes into what you are selling.

Back before calculators, we had to learn long division. If we showed our work, we got partial credit for our effort, even if we didn't come up with the right answer. Show your work to the customer and you'll get the benefit of the doubt when something doesn't go completely right.

In the final analysis, service is specific. It's not dropping by or calling to say, "How is everything going?" It's about adding value with information, strengthening the relationship over a meal or on the golf course, or recognizing a good customer with a thank-you or a perk.

CHAPTER 15

Selling on Purpose *with* Purpose

It was no accident you picked up this book. You were ready to take your career and your income to the next level. Thanks to The Chart (introduced in Chapter 2), you now know what the next level looks like as well as how to get there. It's been my privilege to help show you the way.

Accidental Salesperson Axiom:

Success is not an accident.

Corollary:

Success is a choice.

"Show of hands," I say to the 270 salespeople attending the annual sales meeting I'm addressing. "How many of you in third grade dreamed of becoming a salesperson?" Seldom do more than 2 percent of the audience members raise a hand.

That's why the title of this book has struck such a responsive chord. Just about everyone who sells got into sales accidentally. "That's me," you probably said to yourself when the title caught your eye in a bookstore or online.

So you bought it (thank you!) and now you've actually read it.

In this book I've shown you how to sell on purpose. But I can't tell you how to sell with purpose. I can only ask you this one last question: "Why are you selling, besides for the money?"

Your answer to this question is more important than any Ten Most Wanted List (tool) or use of a magic phrase (tactic). It reveals your deeper purpose, which usually involves being of service to other human beings. That's what drives you. On those days when you don't get your call returned or the sale goes to a competitor, return to your purpose instead of heading for the bar or playing Angry Birds.

When I began my speaking and writing career, I wrote down my purpose: *to make successful people successful sooner.* Here's what I meant: Successful people will figure it out sooner or later, with or without me. They are driven to succeed and so they stick with it. They learn by trial and error, hire a coach, buy books, and attend seminars. The only reason for a company to hire a speaker or buy a training program is so that the people on the team, who are going to succeed anyway, can ramp up their sales six to eighteen months sooner than they would have if they hadn't had the training. That's it. I've always believed that the only reason for salespeople to read this book is to accelerate their success strategy.

Making successful people successful sooner is a purpose I still find very motivating. If I have helped you, I would love to hear about it. You can contact me by e-mail at my website, The AccidentalSalesperson2012.com. Your feedback means a lot. You will be motivating the motivator.

I still recall the time a salesperson came up to me before a seminar and said, "Thank you for my career, Mr. Lytle."

"What do you mean?" I asked.

"My company sent me to your seminar last year. At the time, I had my resignation letter in my desk drawer, but I figured I'd go get the training and then quit," the salesperson said. "But after your seminar, I had a selling system and a way to help my clients get results, too. I tore up the letter, got to work, and am now making more money than I believed possible. I'm very happy. Thank you for my career."

I never tear up over a crisp hundred-dollar bill. But I am tearing up as I recall that moment.

One of my written goals was to write a bestselling business book. I'm told a successful business book sells about 5,000 copies. As you can see by the cover, this book has sold ten times that number. As I wrote the second edition, my goal didn't change, but my purpose evolved. The purpose is to help you, the accidental salesperson, sell on purpose and with purpose, so you can become a "bestseller" in your industry. And to do it sooner than you would have if you hadn't read this book.

Let me know when that happens for you.

Chris Lytle
Chicago
11/11/11

INDEX